# MUSSOLINI AND FASCISM

The early twentieth century in Italy was a crucial period in its history. *Mussolini and Fascism* surveys all the important issues and topics of the period including the origins and rise of Fascism, Mussolini as Prime Minister and dictator, the totalitarian state, foreign policy and the Second World War. It also compares Italian Fascism with other inter-war dictatorships.

**Patricia Knight** is a Senior Lecturer at City and Islington College where she has taught GCSE and A Level history. Her publications include *The Spanish Civil War* (1998).

# QUESTIONS AND ANALYSIS IN HISTORY

Edited by Stephen J. Lee, Sean Lang and Jocelyn Hunt

**Other titles in this series:**

# MUSSOLINI AND FASCISM

## PATRICIA KNIGHT

ROUTLEDGE

London and New York

First published 2003
by Routledge
11 New Fetter Lane, London EC4P 4EE

Simultaneously published in the USA and Canada
by Routledge
29 West 35th Street, New York, NY 10001

*Routledge is an imprint of the Taylor & Francis Group*

© 2003 Patricia Knight

Typeset in Akzidenz Grotesk and Perpetua by
Keystroke, Jacaranda Lodge, Wolverhampton
Printed and bound in Great Britain by
Biddles Ltd, Guildford and King's Lynn

*British Library Cataloguing in Publication Data*
A catalogue record for this book is available from the British Library

*Library of Congress Cataloging in Publication Data*
A catalogue record for this book has been requested

ISBN 0–415–27921–6 (hbk)
ISBN 0–415–27922–4 (pbk)

# CONTENTS

# ILLUSTRATIONS

**PLATES**

**MAPS**

# SERIES PREFACE

Most history textbooks now aim to provide the student with interpretation, and many also cover the historiography of a topic. Some include a selection of sources.

So far, however, there have been few attempts to combine *all* the skills needed by the history student. Interpretation is usually found within an overall narrative framework and it is often difficult to separate the two for essay purposes. Where sources are included, there is rarely any guidance as to how to answer the questions on them.

The Questions and Analysis series is therefore based on the belief that another approach should be added to those which already exist. It has two main aims.

The first is to separate narrative from interpretation so that the latter is no longer diluted by the former. Most chapters start with a background narrative section containing essential information. This material is then used in a section focusing on analysis through a specific question. The main purpose of this is to help to tighten up essay technique.

The second aim is to provide a comprehensive range of sources for each of the issues covered. The questions are of the type which appear on examination papers, and some have worked answers to demonstrate the techniques required.

The chapters may be approached in different ways. The background narratives may be read first to provide an overall perspective, followed by the analyses and then the sources. The alternative method is to work through all the components of each chapter before going on to the next.

# ACKNOWLEDGEMENTS

The author and the publishers wish to thank the following for permission to reproduce copyright material:

Hodder & Stoughton Ltd, for the map of Italy reproduced here as Map 1; Peter Newark's Military Pictures for the photograph of Mussolini reproduced here as Plate 1; Popperfoto for the photograph of Mussolini reproduced here as Plate 2.

Every effort has been made to obtain permission to reproduce copyright material. If any proper acknowledgement has not been made, we would invite copyright holders to inform us of the oversight.

# 1

# LIBERAL ITALY AND THE ORIGINS OF FASCISM

## BACKGROUND NARRATIVE

Following Italian unification in 1870, a Piedmontese statesman commented, 'we have made Italy – now we must make Italians'.[1] This would prove to be a difficult task since unification owed little to Italian nationalist feeling and much more to the diplomacy of the north Italian state of Piedmont and the intervention of foreign powers. Most Italians had played no part in the Risorgimento and were not enthusiastic about the new state. Different regions had little in common and resented the imposition of Piedmontese institutions and customs. Regional dialects were widely spoken (Italian as a language hardly existed outside literature), and illiteracy rates were high.

A striking feature of the new Italy was the contrast between north and south. Northern Italy, with its proximity to the rest of Europe, had seen the beginnings of commercial and industrial activity, together with the emergence of thriving towns and cities. Southern Italy, on the other hand, was overwhelmingly rural, isolated and impoverished. Over much of the provinces of Naples and Sicily bandits, brigands and the mafia continued their depredations largely unchecked. The plight of the south was only partly alleviated by emigration, itself a result of poverty; altogether, between 1870 and 1914 more than five million Italians migrated, mostly bound for the USA or South America, while others went as temporary workers to neighbouring Austria, Switzerland or France.

The new Italian state was a constitutional monarchy with power residing mainly in parliament, though the King (Victor Emmanuel II to 1878, Humbert 1878–1900 and Victor Emmanuel III from 1900) controlled foreign policy and the armed forces and appointed the Senate (the upper house). Members of the Chamber of Deputies came mainly from the landowning and wealthy middle classes. Most described themselves as 'liberals', but they represented regional and local interests rather than political viewpoints, and formed factions around the leading politicians in return for favours or patronage. Till the turn of the century there were no organized political parties. Though governments changed frequently they were mostly permutations of the same small group of politicians, a process known as the *trasformismo* (transformism). Political life was dominated by influential figures such as Agostino Depretis between 1876 and 1887, Francesco Crispi from 1887 to 1896, and Giovanni Giolitti who was Prime Minister for most of the period between 1903 and 1914.

Before 1912 the franchise was very limited. Initially, only about 2 per cent of Italians (mainly the upper and middle class) had the vote, which was restricted by a property tax, an age qualification and literacy tests. The qualifications were relaxed in 1881 but most Italians were still disenfranchised. Politicians were reluctant to grant political rights to a largely illiterate peasant population and not till 1912 was adult male suffrage effectively introduced, when all men who had either passed a literacy test or completed national service were given the vote. Up to 1914 elections were characterized by bribery and intimidation, practices made possible by the small electorate. Most Italians (even those who could vote) took little interest in politics and were alienated by the prevailing corruption and patronage, and the self-interest of politicians.

All post-unification governments had to contend with the hostility of the Roman Catholic Church. Unification, culminating in the occupation of Rome, had deprived the Papacy of its territories (the Papal States) and of political power, and successive popes refused to be reconciled to the new state, preferring to remain 'prisoners in the Vatican'. Liberalism, the creed to which most Italian politicians subscribed, was condemned in the Syllabus of Errors in 1864 and Catholics were forbidden to play any part in politics. Since Catholicism was the religion of the overwhelming majority of Italians, and the clergy wielded considerable influence, especially in rural areas, the

Church's attitude reinforced the prevailing political apathy. The conflict was exacerbated by the anti-clericalism of most Liberal politicians who aimed to reduce the influence of the Church by introducing secular education and civil marriage. This antagonism between Church and state was still largely unresolved in 1914.

Compared with most of western Europe, the Italian economy was underdeveloped in 1870. Italy lacked raw materials such as coal, as well as adequate rail and road communications. In 1871, 70 per cent of the population earned their living in agriculture, and the proportion was still 57 per cent in 1914. Landholdings varied, with some relatively prosperous peasant proprietors in north and central Italy, but most workers on the land were extremely impoverished, the worst-off being the labourers on the large estates, or *latifundia*, in the south.

The economy of southern Italy continued to stagnate, but following unification the north underwent an industrial revolution. In the 1880s, the triangle bounded by Milan, Turin and Genoa experienced a boom in textiles, iron, steel and shipbuilding, the latter underpinned by government expenditure on the navy. The years 1887–95 were marked by a depression with banking failures and financial scandals, but from 1896 industry expanded again.

Industrial development brought with it a larger urban working class and also problems of overcrowded slum housing, long hours of work in factories and poor working conditions. Trade unions had increased their membership to 250,000 by 1900, and in the decade before 1914 social unrest escalated with industrial action culminating in a two-day general strike in the so-called 'red week' in June 1914. In 1892 a Socialist Party (PSI after the Italian initials) was founded, led by Filippo Turati. The left was divided between reformist Socialists, who advocated working legally through parliament, and revolutionaries, anarchists and syndicalists, who favoured direct action, including strikes and demonstrations, to overthrow the government. However, till shortly before the First World War, the reformist Socialists predominated and gained a number of seats in the Chamber of Deputies. Meantime, in the 1890s, partly to counteract Socialism but also in recognition of the need for social reforms, Pope Leo XIII lifted the ban on Catholic participation in politics. This paved the way for the eventual emergence of a Catholic political party (the Popolari, founded at the end of the First World War) and of Catholic trade unions. Most Italian governments countered unrest with repression, but from 1903 Giolitti took a more conciliatory approach, introducing social legislation and observing neutrality in labour disputes. He also attempted to integrate the new groups, the Socialists and Catholics, and on the right wing the Nationalists, into the political system, an experiment still underway in 1914.

Following unification, Italy expected to be treated as a great power, on an equal footing with the other major European states. Its foreign policy was largely determined by relations with France and Austria, the two powers on its northern frontier. A main objective of all Italian governments was to complete the process of unification by acquiring 'unredeemed Italy', Italian-speaking territory in the Tyrol and on the Adriatic coast which was still part of the Austrian empire. Friendship with France was therefore advisable as a counterweight to the Austrians. However, from the 1880s Italian politicians were also intent on colonial expansion, this being the period when possession of an overseas empire was considered an essential prerequisite of great-power status. Conflict with France over Tunisia in North Africa led Italy, in 1882, to join Germany and Austria in the Triple Alliance, which was directed against both France and Russia. This alliance was renewed periodically and was still in existence when war broke out in 1914.

Italy was largely left behind in the scramble for Africa where there was little territory still available. Having failed to acquire Tunisia, it finally obtained a foothold on the East African coast in Somaliland and Eritrea in 1885. It then advanced into Abyssinia, but met with a disastrous defeat by the Abyssinians at the Battle of Adowa in 1896. In 1911 Libya was occupied, the result of an earlier agreement with France.

When, in August 1914, Germany and Austria went to war with Britain, France and Russia, Italy at first remained neutral. It disregarded its alliance with Austria on a technicality but the real reasons were anti-Austrian feeling over 'unredeemed Italy' and fear of naval attack by Britain, on whom the Italians depended for trade and imports of coal. Most deputies and majority public opinion, including Liberals, Catholics and Socialists, were opposed to entering the war. But by 1915 there was a growing vociferous minority of Nationalists and others (including the King) in favour of joining the allied side, arguing that otherwise Italy would be shown to be a second-rate power and would fail to get a share of the spoils. They staged a number of noisy demonstrations and as a result of this 'intervention crisis' Italy entered the war in what the interventionists dubbed 'Radiant May' in 1915. In April it had signed the secret Treaty of London with the Entente powers, by which it was promised Trente, the south Tyrol, Trieste and Dalmatia from Austria, and more vaguely, colonies and territory from the Ottoman Empire.

One of those advocating intervention was Benito Mussolini, at that time a leading member of the revolutionary wing of the Socialist Party. Mussolini was born in 1883 in the Romagna in central Italy. After some unsuccessful attempts at teaching, he eventually became a left-wing agitator and journalist, first in Austrian-ruled Tyrol, then in Forlì in the Romagna where he established himself as a leading revolutionary and opponent of the Libyan war. Mussolini's main talents lay in journalism and in 1912 he moved to Milan to become editor of the main Socialist newspaper, *Avanti*. Initially he followed the Socialist Party line of opposition to the European war but by October 1914 he was advocating intervention, writing: 'Do we wish to be – as men and socialists – inert spectators of this grandiose drama. Or would we prefer to be, in some way, its protagonists?'[2] His change of attitude is explained by Martin Blinkhorn who considers that Mussolini's socialism stemmed from hatred of 'liberal Italy's narrow ruling class as much as the capitalist system, and his goal [was] revolution itself rather than the particular kind of post-revolutionary society desired by most fellow socialists'.[3] Mussolini seems to have seen the war as the precursor to a revolution which would bring the working class to power. In any case he had always favoured violence and direct action over legal methods. But support for the war led to his expulsion from the Socialist Party and loss of his editorship of *Avanti*. Therefore, in 1915 he started a new paper *Popolo d'Italia*, financed both by Italian interventionists and the French government.

The war proved a lot less rewarding for Italy than expected. Militarily, it was not a success; Italian troops made little headway against the Austrians in the Alps and in October 1917 were defeated with great casualties at the Battle of Caporetto, though this was partly reversed in a victory at Vittorio Veneto in the closing stages of the war. Of the 5.9 million Italians conscripted, half a million were killed and one million wounded. Meanwhile, at home, though war industries boomed, most Italians faced food shortages, high prices and falling standards of living.

## ANALYSIS (1): BY 1914 DID THE ITALIAN STATE EXHIBIT MORE WEAKNESSES THAN STRENGTHS?

Italy on the eve of the First World War was not without strengths. The regime had survived for over forty years without serious crisis and some progress had been made in 'making Italians'. The differences between states and regions, so marked in 1871, had been partly broken down, at least in north and central Italy, and steps had been taken to create a national economy with improved road and rail communications. Advances had also been made in education and literacy. The Church had become more conciliatory and Catholics were now allowed to vote and become deputies. Within the limitations of the *trasformismo* system, politics seemed to function reasonably well. After 1912 the franchise compared favourably with that of most other European states at the time. The new forces, Socialists, Catholics and Nationalists, while they threatened to upset the liberal status quo, offered the prospect of a more modern party system and greater political choice.

Though the country as a whole was still largely agricultural, there had been significant expansion of industry in northern Italy, featuring cars, engineering, electricity and chemicals, and the emergence of large firms such as Fiat and Pirelli. True, there were many accompanying social problems, but after 1903 Giolitti had introduced some much needed reforms, for example in improving employment conditions and abolishing child labour; he spent more on public works and took an even-handed approach to industrial disputes. Strikes and social unrest were not necessarily more disruptive or threatening than in other European states at the time and in spite of a lack-lustre foreign and imperial policy, Italy was to be on the winning side in the First World War.

However, these advantages were more than offset by numerous weaknesses. Italy was still in many respects a 'political expression'. In particular, the north–south divide was as great as ever. Unification had, if anything, worsened the plight of the southern provinces by the introduction of heavier taxes and the abolition of internal customs duties which had ruined traditional industries such as silk. Industrial development was largely confined to northern Italy. Illiteracy, which had almost been eliminated in northern Italy by 1914, was still 45 per cent in the south. Successive governments had been unable to address the 'southern problem' successfully.

Quite apart from this, Italy as a whole in 1914 was far from being a modern economy. Most of the population still earned their living on the land. Agriculture depended mainly on cereals and some cash crops such as fruit but, from the 1880s, grain production had suffered from competition from imports from North America. Some modernization had taken place, but traditional agricultural methods were still widely used, especially in the south. In industrial production and other economic indices, Italy lagged well behind most of its neighbours, as can be seen in Source E on p. 12.

Though the Church's attitude had softened, there was still no sign of the fundamental Church–state conflict being resolved by 1914, and there were ongoing disputes over the appointment of bishops and control of schools. Many Italian Catholics continued to hold divided loyalties and did not identify with the state.

It was in the political sphere that Italy's weaknesses were most apparent. Universal male suffrage had come too late to reverse the disillusionment and cynicism with which most Italians viewed the political process. In spite of the emergence of new political groups, notably the Socialists, most deputies in 1914 still represented upper middle-class or regional interests. Patronage was still rife, with votes being sold in return for jobs or favours. Politicians did not command respect and were seen as corrupt and self-serving. The gulf between the 'real' Italy of the mass of the people and 'legal Italy' represented by the government was considerable and communication between them was still 'rare and unfriendly'.[4] Most governments were more interested in survival than in long-term strategies for change or improvement. There had been some attempts to resolve the political malaise as when the right-wing Prime Minister Luigi Pelloux tried to increase the powers of the executive in 1897, but this move was unpopular and came to nothing. There were also attempts at reform by Giolitti after 1903. But these social reforms were too little too late, and failed to appease the working class; welfare benefits, wages and working conditions continued to compare unfavourably with most other west European states. Governments had not resolved the problem of 'how to integrate popular forces into the political and parliamentary processes of the nation'.[5] The *trasformismo* system was ill equipped to deal with social change, but no alternative political system had yet evolved.

The political future was uncertain in 1914, but it seemed likely that the new groups would undermine the Liberals who had dominated Italian politics since 1870. This was apparent in the 1913 election where the Liberals only won a majority by making an electoral alliance with the Catholics. The arrival on the scene in the 1890s of a Socialist Party brought demands for social improvements, which would be difficult to accommodate without alienating the propertied classes. The Socialists were also moving to the left in the years before the war and revolutionary socialists had won a majority at the 1912 PSI Congress. This was partly the result of the recession in the economy after 1907 and of the Libyan war. The occupation of Libya divided Italian opinion: it was welcomed by the Nationalists, and to some extent by the Catholics, but was condemned by most of the left as an imperialist conflict for which working-class conscripts had to pay the price.

Cassels has written that from two factors, 'the gulf between the state and the masses and a national inferiority complex – nearly all of Italy's troubles have stemmed'.[6] It was in foreign and imperial policy that Italy's inferiority complex was most apparent. As the German Chancellor Bismarck commented, it had 'a big appetite but poor teeth'. There was some naval expansion in the 1880s but lack of industrial resources meant that Italy's military capacity was very limited, as was to be revealed in the First World War. She was in fact a second-rate power aspiring to great-power status, derided as 'Italietta' (little Italy) and not taken seriously by the other European powers. The defeat at Adowa in 1896 was a humiliating blow to national pride since Italy was the only European nation to have been beaten by an African people. Few colonies of any value were acquired and the conquest of Libya after 1911 was expensive and tied up Italian forces for several years, as well as creating dissent at home. Membership of the Triple Alliance, entered into largely because of colonial rivalry with France, brought few advantages and meant that claims to 'unredeemed Italy' had to be put into abeyance. Though the alliance persisted till 1914, Italy was in practice unlikely to meet its obligations. The German ambassador to Rome had correctly described Italy in 1905 as 'a pseudo great power . . . nothing but a deadweight on the Triple Alliance'. Italians were aware that their country lacked prestige and governments were blamed for this failure.

There is no doubt that Italy's weaknesses in 1914 were greater than its strengths, but this is not to say that they were sufficient to bring about the collapse of the political system. They help explain why Italy after 1919 was susceptible to Fascism, which promised to end weak government and restore Italian greatness. But they do not explain the emergence and rapid growth of the Fascist movement. Right-wing parties were relatively insignificant in 1914 and the greatest threat to stability seemed to come from the left rather than the right. It required the traumatic impact of war and its aftermath to produce the crisis that caused the demise of the system. Without the war, it seems likely that the Italian parliamentary system would have survived and the country could well have evolved into a modern political democracy.

## Questions

1. What problems were faced by the Italian state in 1914?
2. To what extent had Italian unification succeeded in 'making Italians'?
3. How far had Italy achieved its foreign and imperial policy aims by 1914?

## ANALYSIS (2): TO WHAT EXTENT ARE THE ORIGINS OF FASCISM TO BE FOUND IN PRE-WAR ITALY?

It is impossible to talk about Fascism prior to the First World War, though the word had its origins in pre-war Italy, where the term *fasci*, meaning 'group', was used to describe Sicilian rebels in the 1890s. It was also used to describe workers' organizations and interventionist groups during the war. Only later did Mussolini identify it with the bound rods carried by Roman magistrates, as this was more in keeping with the image he wished to convey of his regime as linked with ancient Rome.

Fascism is a post-First World War phenomenon, but it is possible to detect 'fascist-like ideas'[7] in most European states, including Italy, in the pre-war period. Historians sometimes refer to 'pre-fascism' or 'proto-fascism', meaning a first, incomplete version, to describe the political views that foreshadowed the later Fascist and Nazi movements. In the late nineteenth century over much of Europe the hitherto predominant liberal values came under attack. Where liberalism believed in the rights of the individual and the power of reason and science to bring about progress, the new thinkers emphasized emotion, instinct and the primacy of the race or nation. Writers such as Herbert Spencer in Britain applied Darwin's theories on evolution and the struggle for survival between species to human societies, presupposing a continuous state of conflict between races and nations. These Social Darwinist ideas led to the glorification of war and militarism. Theories of racial superiority were unthinkingly accepted, and were reinforced in the late nineteenth-century period of colonization. Anti-Semitism was prevalent in central Europe, though not in Italy where the proportion of Jews, and especially practising Jews, was small. Whereas representative government was a key liberal tenet, the new thinkers advocated authoritarianism and strong dictatorial leaders. In his writings, the German philosopher, Friedrich Nietzsche, extolled the virtues of great leaders and supermen. And Gustave Le Bon in *The Psychology of Crowds*, written in 1895, emphasized the importance of the nation rather than the individual, and the power of charismatic leaders to sway opinion and control the masses.

These ideas were not solely the preserve of right-wing theorists. Georges Sorel, a French Socialist writer, who advocated revolutionary trade unions and a general strike to overthrow the state, also believed that the masses could be influenced and motivated by inspiring 'myths' rather than by facts or reason. Syndicalism shared some characteristics with right-wing nationalism. From different perspectives, they both opposed parliamentary institutions and promoted violence and direct action as means of achieving their ends. Mussolini was to be influenced by both strands of thought.

In Italy, in the decade before the First World War, a growing number of writers attacked what they saw as ineffective, corrupt government, which they held responsible for Italy's domestic and foreign policy failures. They dwelt on the contrast between the decay of the present system and the former glories of the Roman Empire. Their core beliefs were the necessity of government by strong leaders or elites (as in the writings of the sociologist Vilfredo Pareto), and the revival of Italy as an imperial power.

The most colourful of these writers was Gabriele D'Annunzio, a romantic adventurer, poet and novelist, who 'yearned for heroic leadership, a politics of glory and adventure'.[8] Highly critical of the Italian political system, he envisaged instead 'a leader with burning eyes and strutting chin, standing on a balcony and urging a huge crowd in the piazza below to rebuild the Roman Empire'.[9] This was precisely the oratorical style later assumed by Mussolini, who was to adopt several of D'Annunzio's ideas, including the establishment of paramilitary groups with Blackshirt uniforms.

Equally hostile to the establishment were the futurists. They were a literary and artistic movement founded in 1909 by Filippo Marinetti. Despairing of Italy's unimpressive foreign and colonial record, their manifesto glorified youth, war and violence. It asserted: 'we want to sing of the love of danger, the habit of energy and rashness. . . . The essential elements of our poetry will be courage, audacity and revolt. . . . We want to glorify war – the only cure for the world.' They deplored the fact that Italy was valued only for its historical and artistic heritage, and demanded that it be delivered 'from its gangrene of professors, archaeologists, tourist guides and antiquaries'.[10]

However, these views remained largely confined to the realm of theory. The only Italian right-wing party of any note before 1914 was the Italian Nationalist Association (later to merge with the Fascists), which was founded in 1910 by Enrico Corradini, who had launched a journal *Il Regno* in 1903 and a further publication, *L'Idea Nazionale* in 1911. The disastrous defeat of Italian troops at Adowa had a major impact on

Corradini's thinking. The Nationalists were anti-democratic and anti-socialist and sought to capitalize on what they saw as the Italian 'sense of national inferiority'.[11] They used the analogy of class struggle to apply to nations, arguing that Italy was a 'proletarian nation', exploited by its stronger 'plutocratic' rivals, Britain and France. Calling for a national revival and a successful foreign and imperial policy, the Nationalists were enthusiastic advocates of the Libyan war of 1911–12. One of their supporters, Giovanni Papini, wrote during the war, 'the future needs blood. Italy needs human victims, butchery.' In 1914 he described Italy as 'a country of botched attempts', ruled by 'the old, the incapable, the charlatans'.[12] Another supporter, Alfredo Rocco, advocated a corporate state, with government functions based on economic structures and carried out by representatives of unions and owners, another idea later taken up by Mussolini.

But the Nationalist Party had made little headway by 1914, winning only three seats in the 1913 election. Mussolini was influenced by their views, but historians agree that before the war the Nationalists were 'politically marginal', 'a fringe sub-culture'.[13] In pre-war Italy, the left was more powerful than the right. But the problems resulting from the war made it possible for these 'pre-fascist' ideas to be developed and to attract a much wider audience.

## Question

1. Why did nationalist and anti-liberal movements gain ground in Italy in the years before the First World War?

# SOURCES

### ITALY'S PROBLEMS BEFORE THE WAR

### Source A: Francesco Crispi describes the Italian political system in operation.

You should see the pandemonium at [the Chamber of Deputies] when the moment approaches for an important division. The agents of the government run through the rooms and corridors, to gather votes. Subsidies, decorations, canals, bridges, roads, everything is promised: sometimes an act of justice long denied, is the price of a parliamentary vote.

**Source B: A Socialist deputy, Orazio Raimondo, attacks the Italian political system in 1913.**

The truth is that under a democratic banner we have imperceptibly arrived at a dictatorial regime. The Honourable Giolitti has four times conducted elections, in 1892, 1904, 1909 and 1913. Moreover in his long parliamentary career he has nominated practically all the senators, practically all the councillors of state, all the prefects [local government officials] and all the high officials in our administrative, judicial, political and military hierarchy.... Now, Honourable Giolitti, when parties forget their programmes, when those who arrive at the threshold of the chamber discard the rags of their political convictions at the door, it is necessary to create a majority by other means ... with trickery and corruption. In this way parliamentary institutions are annulled, parties are annihilated, and *trasformismo* ... is achieved.

**Source C: Corruption in elections in the Giolitti era.**

The police enrolled the scum of the constituencies and the underworld of the neighbouring districts. In the last weeks before the polls the opponents were threatened, bludgeoned, besieged in their homes. Their leaders were debarred from addressing meetings, or even thrown into prison until election day was over. Voters ... favouring governmental candidates were given not only their own polling cards, but also those of opponents, emigrants and deceased voters, and were allowed to vote three, five, ten, twenty times.

**Source D: A speech on the principles of nationalism by Enrico Corradini.**

We must start by recognizing that there are proletarian nations as well as proletarian classes; that is to say there are nations whose living conditions are subject to great disadvantage, to the way of life of other nations, just as classes are.... Italy is, materially and morally, a proletarian nation ... [Italy's] institutions are now worn out and her parties all exhausted.

**Source E: The Italian economy in 1913.**

| Country | Share of world manufacturing output (%) | Value of foreign trade (US$billion) | Income per head (US$) |
|---------|------------------|------------------|------------------|
| Britain | 13.6 | 7.5 | 244 |
| Germany | 14.8 | 4.3 | 184 |
| France | 6.1 | 2.2 | 153 |
| Italy | 2.4 | 1.8 | 108 |

## Questions

1. What is meant by *trasformismo* (Source B)? [2]
2. What light do Sources A, B and C shed on the deficiencies of the Italian political system? [6]
*3. What does Corradini mean by his description of Italy as a 'proletarian nation' (Source D)? [4]
4. How does Source E support Corradini's description of Italy as a 'proletarian nation' in Source D? [5]
5. Using all the Sources and your own knowledge, assess the weaknesses of the Italian state in the period before 1914. [8]

## Worked answer

*3. By the description of Italy as 'a proletarian nation' Corradini is using the terminology of class struggle, i.e. conflict between the working and middle classes. By 'materially', he is conveying that Italy is economically worse off than wealthier nations such as Britain and France, as seen in Source E. By 'morally', he means that Italy's prestige, self-esteem and standing have suffered because of its subservient position. Also, he claims, more powerful states have sought to exploit Italy's inferior position and have deprived it of its rightful place in the world, including the opportunity to acquire colonies. This is equivalent to the exploitation of the working class by property owners. He goes on to say that Italy's political institutions have proved incapable of redressing this situation.

# 2

# THE RISE OF FASCISM

## Italy from 1919 to 1922

### BACKGROUND NARRATIVE

After 1919 Italian governments faced numerous problems. The war had lasted longer than anyone had thought possible, with few victories to compensate for the sacrifices made. The outcome of the Peace Conference was particularly disappointing. Italy gained Trente in the Tyrol and Trieste and much of Istria on the Adriatic, but not Fiume, Dalmatia or any colonies in Africa or territory in the Middle East (see Map 1). Most Italians felt their country had been humiliated at Versailles by the more important powers, Britain, France and the USA. It was left to the flamboyant adventurer D'Annunzio to reassert national pride by leading a group of disbanded ex-servicemen to occupy the partly Italian-speaking port of Fiume in September 1919. There, he successfully defied both the Italian government and the allied powers for over a year before being removed.

The war also put great strains on the economy. Government expenditure and the printing of money to pay for the war led to price rises of up to 600 per cent, with a consequent reduction in real incomes, while the collapse of the post-war boom after 1920 resulted in rising unemployment. During and especially after the war, social unrest increased, notably in the *biennio rosso* (two red years) between 1918 and 1920. The Bolshevik seizure of power in Russia in 1917 raised the spectre of a communist revolution, fear of which was

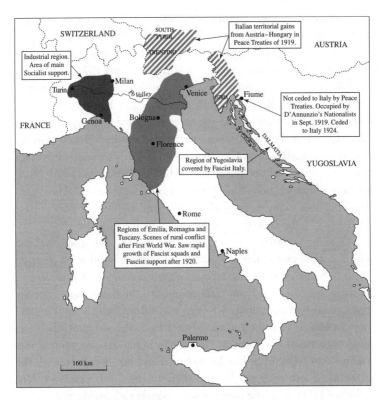

*Map 1* Italy after the First World War
*Source*: M. Robson: *Italy: Liberalism and Fascism 1870–1945* (London: Hodder & Stoughton, 1992)

accentuated by the move to the left of the Socialists and the emergence of the Italian Communist Party in January 1921. Though there was little serious danger of revolution, middle- and upper-class anxieties were reinforced by the government's failure to quell the increasing disorder.

The political context had also changed. Two new political parties, the Socialists (PSI) and the Catholic party (the Popolari), had emerged to challenge the hitherto dominant Liberal bloc. These developments were the result of the politicization of the urban and rural working class and the impact of universal suffrage, introduced just prior to the war. Also, the introduction of proportional representation in 1919, by creating larger constituencies, had made corruption in elections much more difficult. In the November 1919 election the Socialists emerged as the single largest party with 156 seats, while the Popolari (founded in January 1919 and led by a Sicilian priest, Don Luigi Sturzo) gained 100 and the Liberal/Radical bloc 252. After the May 1921 election the Socialists and Communists together numbered 138, the Popolari 108 and Liberals, Radicals and Democrats 233.[1] But the appearance of new parties did not lead to greater political stability, since the three blocs were reluctant to co-operate with one another. Hence, governments continued to be precariously based and short-lived – altogether there were five coalition governments between 1919 and 1922. None of these administrations was equipped to deal with the social problems and conflicts that emerged after 1919 and they were particularly ineffective in the face of the threat posed by the Fascists.

Mussolini served in the army from 1915 to 1917 and, when invalided out, resumed editorship of *Popolo d'Italia* whose subtitle he changed from 'a Socialist daily' to 'a paper of combatants and producers', shifting the emphasis from class conflict to the distinction between those who had contributed to the war effort and those who had not. In March 1919 he set up the first Fascist movement, the Fasci di Combattimento ('Combat Group') in Milan. Its programme was radical and republican but Mussolini could not compete with the established left-wing parties and at first gained little support. Not till after 1920, when he adopted increasingly right-wing and nationalist policies and seized the opportunity offered by agrarian unrest to help farmers and landowners in north and central Italy to resist peasant demands, did the Fascists make any headway. Agrarian Fascism had succeeded, by the end of 1921, in creating a mass movement with a membership of about 200,000.[2] This movement was at first decentralized and loosely organized, run by semi-independent local leaders, called *ras*, after the title of Ethiopian chieftains. Not until November 1921 did Mussolini set up a more structured party.

Meanwhile, in the May 1921 elections, the Fascists had been invited to join Giolitti's National bloc, which gave them thirty-five seats in parliament. Though Fascists were in a small minority in the Chamber of Deputies, Mussolini was now able to pose as a respectable politician while at the same time continuing to encourage the Fascist squads (paramilitary groups composed of ex-soldiers and other disaffected elements) in their violent activities; the squads became increasingly effective in crushing Socialist and other opposition, destroying party headquarters and newspaper offices. Meanwhile, trade union strength declined with the onset of the economic depression: a general strike was called in August 1922 to protest against Fascist violence but it failed.

The Fascists now felt confident of taking power and Mussolini, at a conference in Naples on 24 October 1922, called for a march on Rome by the Blackshirt squads. This was a high-risk strategy, since the police and army were more than capable of crushing the 30,000 or so ill-armed Fascists who were planning to converge on the capital. That the Fascists' bluff succeeded was due to the weakness and vacillation of the King and the politicians on the crucial night of 27/28 October. On 27 October, Victor Emmanuel was persuaded by the Prime Minister, Luigi Facta, to declare a state of emergency, which would have mobilized the army to defend Rome against the squads. But a few hours later, on the morning of 28 October, the King changed his mind. Liberal politicians were equally hesitant and some had been secretly negotiating to bring Mussolini into the government for their own ends. When Facta resigned on 28 October, the King asked another politician, Antonio Salandra, to form a government, but this attempt was abandoned when Mussolini refused to accept any post other than that of Prime Minister. The King then felt he had little alternative but to offer Mussolini the premiership. The Fascist leader arrived in Rome on 30 October, travelling by overnight train from Milan, and the Fascist march (a subdued affair) followed later. Mussolini had come to power by legal means after all, though his success owed much to the turbulence of the previous three years.

## ANALYSIS (1): HOW FAR WAS THE WAR RESPONSIBLE FOR THE CRISIS IN THE ITALIAN STATE BETWEEN 1919 AND 1922?

The war was a major factor in the crisis which beset Italy in this period. First, it greatly intensified the already existing sense of aggrieved nationalism. Though on the winning side, most Italians felt their country had gained little from a war which had resulted in 1.5 million casualties and burdened Italy with debts – the government had borrowed heavily from Britain and the USA to finance the war and the national debt had increased from 16 billion lire in 1914 to 85 billion in 1919; there was also a large budget deficit. The fighting itself had brought little glory and Italian troops had generally performed badly, as illustrated by the defeat at Caporetto in 1917. But the main reason for disillusionment was the peace settlement. At Versailles in 1919, Italy was treated as relatively unimportant and its representatives were outmanoeuvred. The newly formed state of Yugoslavia was awarded most of the Adriatic territory that Italy coveted while Britain and France divided Germany's colonies between them. Italians complained bitterly of a 'mutilated victory'. Italy's grievances were not in fact particularly justifiable since it obtained much of 'unredeemed Italy', but national pride was injured. Governments and politicians were blamed for the fact that Italy had won the war but seemed to have lost the peace. When D'Annunzio seized Fiume in September 1919, he was acclaimed as a popular hero. He was much more famous than Mussolini at this time. The episode illustrated the ineffectiveness of Italian governments when faced with determined paramilitary action, a weakness which the Fascists would later exploit.

Second, the war distorted the Italian economy. It led to a boom in war industries such as engineering, munitions and iron and steel but this was accompanied by unprecedented inflation. Those on fixed incomes suffered most, but real wages also fell. When the boom collapsed after 1920 due to falling demand from war industries, unemployment rose to half a million by 1921. This was less than in more industrialized nations at the time but contributed to feelings of insecurity and to unrest.

A third result of the war was to increase expectations of social change among workers, peasants and soldiers. The two million demobilized soldiers, Mussolini's 'trenchocracy', felt that their efforts had been ill rewarded. They found it hard to adapt to civilian life and many joined paramilitary organizations, including the Fascist Blackshirts. Peasants who had done well out of the war due to rising food prices were emboldened to demand more land, while agricultural labourers went on strike for higher wages and more secure employment. Land occupations had begun during the war on the estates of central Italy and the Po valley and continued afterwards. The government, which during the war had found it expedient to conciliate food producers, tolerated these occupations and legalized them by decrees in 1919 and 1920.

The war and the immediate post-war years also saw a dramatic rise in trade union membership. Membership of Socialist trade unions increased from 250,000 in 1914 to two million by 1920 and Catholic unions from 160,000 to 1.2 million. Rising prices, food shortages, military discipline in factories and prohibition of strikes during the war had all fuelled resentment among industrial workers and led to an upsurge of militancy after 1919. Industrial disputes escalated in the *biennio rosso* between 1918 and 1920, culminating in a large-scale strike in August

1920 when up to 400,000 workers occupied factories (a tactic devised by the socialist writer, Antonio Gramsci) in towns and cities across northern Italy, including Milan and Turin. Factory organizations were set up which seemed very similar to Russian soviets. The occupations ended peaceably with a compromise settlement, but not before they had spread great alarm among industrialists, who observed that the government took little action against the strikers.

A fourth factor brought about by the war was indeed the much greater fear of revolution among the propertied classes. The Bolshevik seizure of power in Russia, combined with growing social unrest at home, convinced many of the upper and middle class that revolution was imminent. A major cause for alarm was the much greater electoral support obtained by the Socialists, who not only emerged as the largest single party in the 1919 election but also, under the impact of the war and the Russian Revolution, became, in rhetoric at least, more revolutionary. The 1920 local elections, on a reformed system of local government, also brought the Socialists to power in town councils over much of north and central Italy; altogether, they controlled one-quarter of all local councils. These councils raised taxes, spent more on public services, promoted cooperatives and supported higher wages for agricultural workers. To many property owners, including small landowners and tenant farmers, this looked very much like the inauguration of Bolshevism.

The revolutionary threat was in fact largely unfounded since the Communists were few in number and the Socialists lacked a viable strategy. The Socialist Party had little intention of taking any extra-parliamentary action, expecting the system to collapse of its own accord; as a headline in *Avanti* in November 1919 put it, 'all we have to do is wait'.[3] The Communist Party split from the Socialists in 1921, and this had the effect of dividing and weakening the left. The factory occupations were in fact the high point of industrial militancy, which declined with the collapse of the post-war boom after 1921. But the damage had already been done. Many of the propertied classes now lived in dread of a Communist take-over and, given the passivity of Italian governments, which as in the pre-war period chose to remain neutral in labour disputes, they increasingly looked to the Fascists to prevent it. Fear of Bolshevism combined with the myth of a 'mutilated victory' have been identified as the two factors brought about by the war which most contributed to push Italy 'into the embrace of Fascism'.[4]

Last, the political system after 1919 was further discredited by the inability of governments to deal with these post-war economic and social problems. Italy's difficulties were not unique; they were common to most European nations which had participated in the war, with the difference that Italian governments were less equipped than most to resolve them. In particular they seemed impotent to deal with the unrest in town and countryside, impose law and order or curb Fascist violence. Also, unlike other European states, Italy had no effective right-wing parties to provide an alternative to the Fascists.

However, the war alone is insufficient to account for Italy's crisis. Longer-term factors were also responsible. Many of Italy's political, social and foreign policy problems, as seen in chapter 1, dated from before the war. Frustrated nationalism had existed for many years before 1919, though the peace settlement greatly aggravated it. Social unrest was apparent before 1914, as were the weaknesses of the political system. The crucial factor, however, was that these political weaknesses were not remedied in the post-war period. The emergence of new parties did not lead to greater political stability, since these new groups proved unwilling to work together to create effective government. The Socialists refused to participate in Liberal-led governments, which weakened the political system, while the Popolari, though in favour of moderate social reform, were opposed to both the Socialists (whom they identified with atheistic communism) and the anti-clerical Liberals. Socialists and Catholics were too ideologically opposed to join forces. The Popolari in turn were divided between a right and a left wing and the Liberals were split into several different factions. It is not therefore surprising that post-war governments failed to resolve Italy's crisis or to withstand the Fascist threat.

## Questions

1. Why in the period 1919–22 did Italian democracy prove so fragile?
2. Why was there a crisis in government by 1922?

## ANALYSIS (2): HOW WAS MUSSOLINI, THE LEADER OF AN INSIGNIFICANT GROUP IN 1919, ABLE TO BECOME PRIME MINISTER THREE YEARS LATER?

Having cut his ties with the Socialists, Mussolini counted for little and the end of the war found him 'stranded on the margins of Italian political life'.[5] Only 188 people were present at the first meeting of the Fasci di Combattimento in Milan in March 1919, mainly interventionists, ex-Socialists, syndicalists and war veterans. The position by the end of the year was no different. The Fascists had only 4,000 members and obtained few votes and no seats in the November 1919 election.

Mussolini's supporters represented a wide range of political views but the Fascist programme of 1919, though nationalist, was still very radical, anti-monarchist and anti-clerical. It advocated votes for women, abolition of the Senate, nationalization of armaments factories, a tax on capital, a minimum wage, an eight-hour day and confiscation of the property of religious organizations. But these left-wing policies were disadvantageous since the Fascists were quite unable to compete with the much better-established Socialists, while on the right Mussolini was relatively unknown. He seemed very far from taking power.

However, the Fascists were to benefit from a number of factors, namely fear of Bolshevism, industrial and agrarian unrest, and the ineffectiveness of Italian governments. Mussolini also proved skilful at adapting his ideas and tactics to changed circumstances. When it became clear that there was nothing to be gained from left-wing views, these were dropped, and soon the Fascists were supporting the propertied classes and the Church. Mussolini also abandoned republicanism, realizing that to win power he would need the acquiescence of the King. Fascism's main ideas, notably support for strong government and the regeneration of Italy as a powerful nation, undoubtedly appealed to the large number of Italians who were tired of weak governments and foreign policy failures. However, Fascism at this time was more negative than positive; it was easier to identify what it was against, such as socialism, communism, liberalism and democracy, than what it stood for. As later recounted by Mussolini, '[Fascism] was born of the need for action and . . . was not merely another political party but . . . in opposition to all political parties as such and itself a living movement.'[6] The imprecise and emotive nature of Fascist ideology at this time is also illustrated by his statement that 'Doctrine . . . might be lacking . . .' but had been substituted by 'something more decisive – Faith.'[7] But that Fascism was a movement rather than an organized party, and seemed to lack coherent or consistent policies, was not necessarily a drawback, since it was thus able to diversify its appeal to suit different audiences.

Mussolini also brought personal assets to bear in his quest for power, notably his popular journalistic and oratorical skills; he reinforced his leadership of the movement mainly by his hold over the party newspaper *Popolo d'Italia*. He was helped by the fact that D'Annunzio, his chief potential rival on the right, had retreated into obscurity after abandoning his occupation of Fiume in 1920. But Mussolini found it useful to appropriate many aspects of D'Annunzio's style: blackshirted uniforms, the Roman salute and the practice of making rousing speeches to admiring crowds.

Fear of communism was a major factor in the rise of Fascism. From autumn 1920 the Fascists were able to fill the vacuum left by government inaction by supporting landowners and farmers who were threatened by peasant leagues in northern and central Italy and feared to lose their property in land occupations. Many of the Fascist activists were demobilized soldiers, including *arditi* (elite forces during the war), who formed themselves into armed squads and proceeded to terrorize the countryside. Often financed by local farmers and businessmen who provided transport and weapons, the squads carried out punitive expeditions against trade unions and Socialist organizations, attacking and burning down headquarters and newspaper offices. Between 1920 and 1922, 200 people were killed, and many more injured or forced, often with the help of the authorities, police and army, to drink copious quantities of castor oil. By 1921 agrarian Fascism enabled Mussolini to command a mass movement in north and central Italy, though there was much less activity or support in the south. Fascists also took advantage of urban unrest in the *biennio rosso*, especially with the threat of revolution implicit in the factory occupations of 1920. Responding to middle-class fears, they attacked strikers and Socialist town councils. The Socialists fought back but were generally no match for the squads.

As a result of these activities Fascism grew in strength. From about 20,000 in the summer of 1920, membership increased to 200,000 by the end of 1921 and up to 300,000 by October 1922. It appealed particularly to the middle or lower middle class – farmers, tradesmen, white-collar workers, public employees, professional men and the self-employed; workers comprised only a minority of the membership. The movement successfully projected an image of dynamism and youthful-ness, a characteristic of Fascism in this period being the youth of its members, while 'Giovinezza' ('Youth') was the Fascist anthem.

However, despite these advantages, it is unlikely that Mussolini could have come to power without the connivance of established politicians or the mistakes of other parties. He benefited as much from the weak-nesses of the Italian political system as from his own efforts. Italian governments abetted Mussolini by failing to enforce law and order or to take action against Fascist violence. The police and the army often aided the Fascists, or at best stood on the sidelines. The Italian authorities hoped to use Mussolini to crush the left and believed that communism was a greater threat than Fascism, the implications of which they did not understand.

A significant breakthrough had occurred when Giolitti invited the Fascists to join his national bloc in the May 1921 elections. Giolitti felt he needed the Fascists to form a stable government; he discounted Mussolini's anti-democratic pronouncements and thought he could control him. As he said, 'The Fascist candidates will be like fireworks.

They will make a lot of noise but will leave nothing behind except smoke.'[8] This error of judgement gave Fascism a foothold in parliament and made it look respectable and legitimate. It provided Mussolini with a platform for his views and an opportunity to exploit government weaknesses. Henceforth he was able to pursue simultaneously the twin tactics of legal action and violence. Mussolini thus benefited from the mistakes of politicians who wished to cooperate with the Fascists for their own ends.

The Socialists, too, played into the hands of the Fascists by advocating social changes which they had little intention or means of carrying out. They also contributed to political instability by refusing to participate in governments or to cooperate with other parties. Trade union tactics were also unwise. In August 1922 a general strike was called to protest against Fascist violence but by this time trade unions were less powerful: the strike was only partially supported and it collapsed after twenty-four hours. Its failure gave the Fascists a further boost.

However, Mussolini's rise to power was not without its difficulties. For one thing, he was in danger of losing control of Fascism to the semi-independent *ras* who were very much a law unto themselves. As one Fascist put it, 'every region, every province, possesses its own Fascism'.[9] This regionalized nature of Fascism enabled local bosses such as Roberto Farinacci in Cremona, Dino Grandi in Bologna, Italo Balbo in Ferrara and Carlo Scorza in Lucca to be almost as powerful as Mussolini himself. In summer 1921, for example, they successfully prevented him from arranging a truce with Socialists designed to reduce the Fascist violence which Mussolini feared was alienating the Liberal politicians. This was a setback and Mussolini did not regain his authority until the establishment of a more structured Fascist Party (Partito Nazionale Fascista or PNF) in November 1921. Even after this, he was still dependent on the *ras* and *squadristi* for support.

Nor did Mussolini in the summer of 1922 (unlike Hitler in 1933) have a substantial base in parliament, so there was no constitutional reason why he should have become Prime Minister. His call for a march on Rome in October 1922 was designed partly to capitalize on the success of the squads in much of north and central Italy where they recently had taken over many towns (including Milan), but also to forestall the possible emergence of an anti-Fascist front in parliament. However, when on 24 October at the Fascist conference in Naples he threatened: 'either they will give us the government or we shall seize it by descending on Rome',[10] this was largely a bluff. It was the *ras* who were responsible for organizing the march. Four Quadrumvirs, including the militia leaders Balbo, Cesare De Vecchi and Emilio De Bono, together with the party secretary Michele

Bianchi, planned the seizure of key buildings such as police stations, communications centres and post offices on the night of 27 October, before advancing on the capital. However, the police and army were more than sufficient to deal with the relatively small and ill-armed *squadristi*. Mussolini, apparently uncertain of success, prudently remained in Milan, ready to escape across the frontier in the event of failure.

The Fascists succeeded because both the King and the politicians were prepared to bring Mussolini into government. A state of virtual civil war existed over much of north and central Italy and the government was in disarray. The King, described as a 'tiny and timid creature', was irresolute, first agreeing to a state of emergency on 27 October and then changing his mind a few hours later. Victor Emmanuel seems to have acted for a variety of reasons, including fear of being deposed in favour of his pro-Fascist cousin the Duke of Aosta and fear of civil war (explanations for his decision are explored in the Sources at the end of this chapter).

But the King did not bear all the responsibility; other politicians including Giolitti also wished to invite Mussolini into the government, hoping that this would neutralize the Fascists and stabilize the political system. However, Mussolini refused to serve in a Salandra-led government and held out for the post of Prime Minister. These tactics succeeded and Mussolini finally arrived in Rome on 30 October not at the head of a Fascist march but by overnight sleeper. In the last resort he had not taken power but been given it by politicians who were not averse to using him for their own ends. 'Despite the "revolutionary" myth of the Fascist March on Rome in October 1922, it is true to say that Fascism owed its accession to power largely to conservative forces.'[11]

## Questions

1. Was it the weakness of the opposition rather than the strength of the Fascists which enabled Mussolini to become Prime Minister in 1922?
2. Describe the main stages by which Fascism developed into an effective political movement between March 1919 and the march on Rome in October 1922.
3. Why was Mussolini appointed Prime Minister in 1922?

# SOURCES

## 1. THE DEVELOPMENT OF FASCIST IDEAS AND TACTICS 1919–22

### Source A: The June 1919 Fascist programme.

Universal suffrage ... with votes for women and their eligibility for office
Abolition of the Senate
... the 8 hour working day
Minimum pay
The nationalization of all arms and munitions factories ...
A heavy, extraordinary and progressive tax on capital which involves a meaningful partial expropriation of all forms of wealth
The confiscation of all property belonging to religious organizations
The revision of all arms contracts and the confiscation of 85 per cent of war profits.

### Source B: Mussolini's first speech in Parliament, 21 June 1921.

Honourable colleagues, I am not unhappy to be delivering my speech from the benches of the extreme right ... in its substance it will be clearly anti-democratic and anti-socialist ... if you present a bill for the eight-hour day, we shall vote for it. . . . We shall not oppose; indeed, we shall vote in favour of all measures intended to improve our body of social legislation. . . . But let me warn you at once that we shall resist with all our strength any attempt at socialization, collectivism and state socialism! . . . Fascism does not preach and does not practise anti-clericalism ... I believe and affirm that the Latin and Imperial traditions of Rome are today represented by Catholicism ... and that the sole universal idea that exists in Rome is that which radiates from the Vatican.

### Source C: Balbo (a squad leader) describes Fascist violence in summer 1922

I [then] announced to [the chief of police] that I would burn down and destroy the houses of all Socialists in Ravenna if he did not give me within half an hour the means required for transporting the Fascists elsewhere. It was a dramatic moment. I demanded a whole fleet of trucks. The police officers completely lost their heads; but after half an hour they told me where I could find trucks already filled with gasoline. Some of them actually belonged to the office of the chief of police. My ostensible reason was that I wanted to get the exasperated Fascists out of town; in reality, I was organizing a 'column of fire' ... to extend our reprisals throughout the province. . . . We went through ... all the towns and centres in the provinces of Forlì and Ravenna and burned all the Red buildings. . . . It was a terrible night. Our passage was marked by huge columns of fire and smoke.

## Source D: The Proclamation of the Quadrumvirate, 26 October 1922, issued just before the planned march on Rome.

Fascists! Italians! The time for determined battle has come! Four years ago the National Army loosed at this season the final offensive, which brought it to victory. Today the army of the Blackshirts takes again possession of that victory, which has been mutilated, and going directly to Rome brings victory again to the glory of that capital. . . . The Army, the reserve and the safeguard of the Nation, must not take part in their struggle. Fascism renews its highest homage given to the Army of Vittorio Veneto.

## Source E: Mussolini looks back on his rise to power (from 'The doctrine of Fascism', *Enciclopedia italiana*, 1932).

The years preceding the March on Rome cover a period during which the need for action did not tolerate inquiries or complete elaborations of doctrine. . . . Battles were being fought in the cities and villages. There were discussions but – and this is sacred and important – there were deaths. People knew how to die. . . . Nevertheless . . . the foundations of doctrine were laid while the battle was raging . . . the problems of the individual and the State; the problems of authority and liberty; political, social and those more specifically national; the struggle against liberal, democratic, socialistic, Masonic . . . doctrines and with those of the 'Partito Popolare', was carried on at the same time as the 'punitive expeditions'.

## Questions

1. Explain the references in Source D to 'Vittorio Veneto' and 'victory which has been mutilated'. [4]
*2. Compare Mussolini's views in Source B with the Fascist programme in Source A. [5]
3. What evidence is there in Source C to show that the police connived at Fascist violence? [4]
4. How far do Sources C and E support the claim that Fascism was a negative and violent movement? [6]
5. In what ways, in Source D, did the Quadrumvirate seek to conciliate the army? Using your own knowledge, explain why it was necessary to do this in October 1922. [6]

## Worked answer

*2. In Source A Mussolini is putting forward a radical political and social programme including legislation for an eight-hour day, a minimum wage, some nationalization and attacks on war profits. Source A is also extremely anti-clerical. This programme was similar to that of the Socialists. In Source B, anti-clericalism has been completely abandoned. Mussolini now found it expedient to conciliate the Church and went out of his way to extol the Papacy: 'the sole universal idea that exists in Rome is that which radiates from the Vatican'. In his 1921 speech, he announces that he is speaking from a right-wing and anti-democratic perspective, implying that he has also changed his views on democracy and votes for women.

Mussolini wanted to preserve some of his left-wing credentials, so in Source B there is qualified support for social legislation but it is distinctly less enthusiastic than in Source A and includes the caveat that there must be no question of state socialism – so contradicting the points in Source A regarding nationalization and expropriation of property.

# SOURCES

## 2. VICTOR EMMANUEL'S ROLE IN MUSSOLINI'S APPOINTMENT AS PRIME MINISTER

### Source F: A historian explains Victor Emmanuel's actions.

What of Victor Emmanuel III . . .? For him the best pressure was to hint that his cousin, the Duke of Aosta, was taller, a better soldier and could make a more manly king. . . . The main politicians eyed each other but could not unite. Salandra, Orlando and Giolitti each awaited his own return to the Prime Ministership, but each indicated a preference that the post be entrusted to the young Mussolini rather than a hated rival. . . . The Vatican washed its hands. Facta fluffed an effort to impose martial law.

### Source G: Another historian's view of Mussolini's appointment.

There have been many attempts to explain the King's action. Diaz and other leading generals are supposed to have indicated that 'the army will do its duty but it would be better not to put it to the test'; rumours of a 'plot' to replace the King with his pro-Fascist first cousin the Duke of Aosta are believed to have influenced his decision, and northern industrialists like Silvio Crespi and Antonio Benni voiced their opposition to a confrontation with Fascism. These are all valid explanations. The

King was not a forceful character but he was quite shrewd and must have realized rapidly that there was no consensus in favour of a showdown with Mussolini. All the leading politicians favoured accommodation and that included Facta himself; the generals, the prefects, industrial magnates and landowners, newspaper editors . . . and the church all had great reservations about any move which might create even more disorder and destruction, leaving Italy at the mercy of the subversives of the left. To preserve his throne and to prevent civil war, the King backed down, accepted Facta's resignation and asked Salandra to form a new government.

### Source H: A further view of the King's decision.

by 9 a.m. [on 28 October] it became known that the King had unaccountably changed his mind . . . His motives must be guessed. No doubt he wanted to avoid bloodshed, but in that case it is incredible that he did not consult General Pugliese who was confident that the insurrection would collapse with perhaps no bloodshed at all. Probably he had decided to get rid of the feeble Facta, relying on his knowledge that Salandra had already agreed to form a government that included Mussolini and excluded Giolitti. Almost certainly the King wanted to avoid appointing Giolitti. . . . The King is also known to have feared that unless he gave way, the Fascists were intending to dethrone him and put Aosta in his place. Though he insisted that the decision to reject martial law was taken personally by himself, he was certainly influenced by mysterious visitors or telephone conversations in the early hours of the 28th. . . . The officers on duty at the palace would certainly have influenced his decision and, though the fact was denied, Diaz apparently sent him advice that the army might be unreliable.

### Source I: A historian comments on Victor Emmanuel's post-Second World War explanation for his decision to appoint Mussolini.

The explanations which Victor Emmanuel gave of his refusal to sign the emergency decree in 1945 are vitiated by their purpose as Royalist propaganda; and all his retrospective statements, indeed, are marked by a desire to put his decision in the best light possible. . . . The excuse that he quite literally ceded to *force majeure*, convinced that the garrison of Rome was too small and too unreliable to resist the Fascist attack, will not hold. However, some part of these several statements may be helpful in understanding the King's state of mind: 'At difficult moments everyone is capable of indecision . . . few or none are those who can take clear decisions and assume great responsibilities. In 1922 I had to call "these people" to the government because all the others, in one way or another, had abandoned me'; on other occasions the King spoke of his desire to 'avoid bloodshed given the news from the provinces which were already in the hands of the Fascists', and he said that if he had acted otherwise, 'it would have been civil war'.

## Questions

1.  Who were Facta and Giolitti (Sources F and H)? [2]
2.  How far do Sources F, G and H agree on the reasons for the King's appointment of Mussolini as Prime Minister? [7]
3.  Using your own knowledge, explain why 'industrial magnates . . . landowners . . . and the church' (Source G) all favoured an accommodation with Mussolini. [5]
4.  Why, after the Second World War would Victor Emmanuel wish to 'put his decision in the best light possible' (Source I)? [4]
*5. How convincing is Victor Emmanuel's post-war explanation (Source I) for his decision to appoint Mussolini? Use all the Sources in your answer. [7]

## Worked answer

*5. *[This is a substantial answer bringing in material from all Sources and you need to compare Victor Emmanuel's reasons with those put forward by historians.]*

After Mussolini's fall from power, Victor Emmanuel was understandably eager to dissociate himself from the Fascist regime. He wished to disclaim responsibility, as far as possible, for Mussolini's appointment. He therefore chose to put the blame on others, the politicians who 'had abandoned me'. He also asserted that the army was unreliable and incapable of repulsing the Fascist march, but, as the commentary in Source I points out, this is not really a viable argument, though the King might have been persuaded otherwise, as suggested in Sources G and H. Victor Emmanuel, however, exaggerated the power of the Fascists and the likelihood of civil war and bloodshed had he refused Mussolini. He portrayed himself as having had no choice, or alternatively as acting disinterestedly to save the nation from further disorder.

There are some elements of truth in the King's explanation. While the politicians had not exactly 'abandoned' him, it is true that leading politicians (and other powerful interests including the Vatican), as stated in Sources F and G, favoured bringing Mussolini into government and gave the King unhelpful advice. But the King's explanation leaves out many other factors. He was nowhere near as disinterested as he makes out in Source I. He omits to mention that a major reason for his decision was fear of being deposed in favour of his cousin (Sources F, G and H). The reason he feared civil war was that it might result in his own downfall. Also he does not mention the political intrigues among the politicians or the possible motives to remove Facta and out-manoeuvre Giolitti (Sources F and H).

The King's account therefore is selective and to this extent unconvincing. It is unlikely that he was unaware of the ability of the army to defeat the Fascists, though he may have doubted its reliability. Source H implies that he was likely to have consulted a leading commander, General Pugliese, on this point. Though the King was a weak character and often took the line of least resistance, he may not have been as passive a participant as he suggests. It is more probable that because he feared the left, he, too, was not averse to bringing Mussolini into government and did not realize the implications of this till too late.

# 3

# FROM PRIME MINISTER TO DICTATOR, 1922 TO 1926

## BACKGROUND NARRATIVE

Mussolini had never made any secret of his desire for complete power, but in October 1922 he was some way from achieving this ambition. He was the Prime Minister of a coalition government, which included only four Fascist ministers out of a total of fourteen, the remainder being Nationalists, Liberals, Democrats and Popolari. Mussolini, however, took over the Interior and Foreign ministries and De Bono, a leading Fascist, became chief of police; Fascists were also more numerous below cabinet level in key under-secretary posts.

In the Chamber of Deputies Mussolini still had only thirty-five seats out of a total of 535 and the merger with the Nationalists in February 1923 only increased this number to forty-seven. To acquire dictatorial powers he had to win a majority in the Chamber and eliminate or neutralize non-Fascist parties. To conciliate conservative interest groups he also had to restrain the extremists in the Fascist Party, and make the party itself more manageable.

In November 1922 Mussolini acted quickly to persuade parliament to grant him emergency powers to introduce legislation by decree for one year. This was not a new device and had been used frequently since 1870 to avert parliamentary crises. Then, in December 1922, the Fascist Grand Council was established which gave Mussolini greater control over the *ras*; in January 1923 the Fascist squads were reorganized in a militia answerable only to Mussolini, thus providing him with a 300,000-strong private army which could also act as a counterweight to the regular army and the police.

A majority in parliament was essential before Mussolini could make progress towards a dictatorship. But before calling elections he needed to be certain of success. Hence, in July 1923 the Chamber was prevailed upon to pass the Acerbo Law (named after the deputy who proposed it), which stated that the party which obtained the largest number of votes in an election, provided these were in excess of 25 per cent of the total, would get two-thirds of the seats. Mussolini was confident that the Fascists could obtain the required percentage. In the election held in April 1924 his expectations were exceeded when the Fascists and their allies received two-thirds of the votes, winning 375 seats in all. The result somewhat overstated Mussolini's popularity since it was partly achieved by use of violence, intimidation and corruption, and only 7.5 million of the 12 million voters actually voted; Mussolini's list also included many liberal-conservatives, who used their local influence in favour of the Fascist bloc. However, the Fascists now enjoyed a huge majority over the opposition parties since the Popolari had won only thirty-nine seats, the Socialists forty-six and the Communists nineteen.

With the election over, it looked as if nothing could now stand in Mussolini's way, but in fact he was on the verge of a crisis which almost resulted in his downfall. On 30 May, a prominent Socialist, Giacomo Matteotti, spoke out in the Chamber against the corruption and fraud which had characterized the election and tried to have it declared invalid. On 10 June he was kidnapped and stabbed to death. His body was not discovered till August, but the kidnapping had already become a major political scandal. An attack on a deputy was tantamount to an attack on the parliamentary system itself and Matteotti was a well-known and respected figure. More importantly, the car used in the kidnap was located and the crime traced back to Mussolini's closest colleagues. The ringleader was Amerigo Dumini, the organizer of a gang (nicknamed the Cheka after the Soviet secret police) which operated from the Ministry of the Interior. Implicated in the murder, and possibly having authorized it, were Cesare Rossi, the head of Mussolini's press bureau (where Dumini was an assistant), and Giovanni Marinelli, a senior official in the Fascist Party.[1] It was alleged that Mussolini himself was involved. It is not known how far he was responsible for the actual killing, as opposed to the cover-up. Certainly he had never made any secret of his wish to have life made difficult for opponents. After Matteotti's speech Mussolini was heard to remark: 'That man, after that speech, should not be allowed to go around.'[2]

As a consequence of the Matteotti murder, public opinion began to turn against Mussolini. Some leading Fascists such as De Bono (head of the militia), Aldo Finzi (Under-Secretary at the Ministry of the Interior) and Rossi were obliged to resign. And in a further move to conciliate his conservative allies, Mussolini was obliged to hand the Interior Ministry over to the Nationalist, Luigi Federzoni. But this was insufficient to quell the opposition. At the end of June, a hundred deputies, led by the Liberal Giovanni Amendola and including Socialists and Popolari, withdrew from parliament in protest, a move known as the Aventine secession after a similar event in ancient Rome. The months between June and November only provided a breathing space for Mussolini. While still facing accusations of complicity in Matteotti's murder, he was beset with demands from the more extreme Fascists for an immediate dictatorship. In November, Balbo, who had succeeded De Bono as head of the militia, also had to resign after allegations that he was responsible for attacks on Socialists.

When parliament resumed in November, prominent politicians such as Giolitti and Salandra withdrew their support from Mussolini, and the Senate appeared likely to follow suit. On 27 December Amendola's newspaper published the 'Rossi Memorandum'. Rossi, one of those arrested for Matteotti's killing, feared he was being made a scapegoat for the murder and his statement accused Mussolini of ordering attacks on opponents, though not on Matteotti. Admittedly, the holiday period was not the best time for the memorandum's publication, but it added to the pressure on Mussolini and his fate hung in the balance. For some months he had wavered between promising 'normalization' of politics on the one hand and encouraging the more extreme Fascists, militia and *ras* on the other. But at the end of December he finally opted for the latter. His resolve was stiffened by the visit of thirty-three consuls (militia leaders) on 31 December, ostensibly to deliver New Year greetings but really to warn Mussolini that unless he reasserted his authority they would withdraw their support. Mussolini had probably already decided on this course of action and had persuaded the cabinet on 30 December to agree measures against the critics of the government.[3] But the consuls' visit confirmed his determination to take a firm line and crush the opposition. On 3 January 1925 he made a momentous speech to the Chamber, taking responsibility for the events of the previous few months, though not for Matteotti's death, and promising strong government. This speech was quickly followed by mobilization of the militia and concerted attacks on opposition groups. Mussolini's enemies had missed their opportunity and, with the crisis behind him, the way was now open to move to a dictatorship.

Four attempts on Mussolini's life in 1925 and 1926 provided pretexts for further repression. Opponents were harassed or forced into exile. Most Communist leaders had already been arrested and in October 1925 the reformist Socialists were banned. By November 1926 all the opposition parties had been dissolved and Italy became a one-party state. After 1924, elected local councils were replaced by prefects who were appointed from above and were reliable supporters of the regime.

With the cabinet exclusively Fascist and parliament subdued, only the press remained as an avenue for opposition. Mussolini took a great interest in journalism and personally monitored the Fascist *Popolo d'Italia*, but in 1922 this sold few copies compared with better-established and more reputable papers such as *Corriere della Sera*, *La Stampa* and *Il Mondo*. There was also the Socialist *Avanti*, and the Communist *L'Unità*. In July 1924 a press law had given prefects the power to warn or dismiss editors who disseminated 'false news', injured 'the national honour' or excited 'disobedience to laws'.[4] The December 1925 press law stated that only registered journalists could write, but censorship was also effected by buying out proprietors or putting pressure on them to remove intransigent editors. Influence was also exerted on foreign journalists, ensuring a largely favourable press abroad.

The decisive move to dictatorship came in December 1925 when the title of Head of Government was conferred on Mussolini. This gave him a vastly elevated role. Henceforth, he was responsible only to the King, the cabinet was demoted to a consultative position, and parliament could discuss nothing without his permission. The November 1926 Decree on Public Security gave prefects power over individuals who were considered to threaten the state. Many opponents were exiled abroad or to remote parts of Italy. Also, in 1926 a Law for the Defence of the State set up military courts, with no jury or right of appeal, to try political crimes. A secret police (OVRA) was also established.

Mussolini's power was not absolute. In theory the King could dismiss him, and the Senate, the army and the Church remained relatively independent. In spite of some attempts to purge them, institutions such as the civil service continued to function largely as before. But there was little doubt that by the end of 1926 Mussolini had succeeded in destroying the Italian constitution and had replaced it with a dictatorship.

## ANALYSIS: WHAT FACTORS ASSISTED MUSSOLINI IN HIS ESTABLISHMENT OF A DICTATORSHIP?

In October 1922 it was not inevitable that Fascism would prevail. Fascists were in a minority in the government and in the Chamber. The merger with the Nationalists in 1923 benefited Mussolini by providing him with closer links with the establishment, the monarchy, the army and the upper class, together with greater intellectual coherence, but it did not provide many more seats. It was the weakness of the opposition as well as Mussolini's own strategy which would enable him to consolidate his position.

Mussolini had stated in a speech in September 1922 at Udine: 'Our programme is simple: we want to govern Italy.'[5] But to achieve this, he had to maintain a balance between his conservative allies and the revolutionaries in the Fascist Party (itself divided into factions) who were impatient to overthrow the old ruling class and to utilize the squads in pursuit of a 'second revolution'. Now that Mussolini was Prime Minister, the extremists in the Fascist Party posed a potential threat to his position. Membership had expanded from 300,000 in October 1922 to 783,000 by the end of 1923, and elements in the party, including powerful figures such as Farinacci and Balbo who saw the march on Rome as the prelude to an immediate dictatorship, were frustrated at not receiving the rewards and offices they had expected. Mussolini needed the *ras* and their followers to intimidate his enemies and numerous people were injured or killed by the squads in the first few months of his administration. But equally, he needed to bring them under his control, in order not to alarm his conservative allies in parliament. Mussolini used the Fascist Grand Council both to counterbalance the cabinet and to increase his influence over the *ras*, since he decided when it should meet, and he set the agenda and co-opted the members. Organizing the *squadristi* into a Fascist militia (which swore an oath to Mussolini) was another useful step towards domination of the party.

A major reason for Mussolini's success lay in the complacency and divisions of the other political parties, most of which preferred to discount his dictatorial ambitions. Mussolini certainly made no secret of his contempt for parliament. In his first speech as Prime Minister, he declared, 'I could have made a bivouac of this gloomy hall; I could have shut up parliament and formed a government only of Fascists. I could have done this, but I did not wish to do so, at any rate at the moment.'[6] At this time he did not in fact have the power that this statement implied, but none of the politicians, except Socialists and Communists, seemed alarmed by the speech or by the emergency decree powers Mussolini was granted. Giolitti's response was that the Chamber had 'got the government it deserves'.[7] Most Liberals hoped, against the evidence, that Fascism could be 'normalized' and made into an ordinary political party. In any case the Liberals were weaker than before the war; the provincial towns and old-established cities, which had been their main source of support, had become less important as a result of industrialization,[8] and they had also lost out to the new political parties.

Of these new parties, the Popolari were at first inclined to oppose the Fascists, on account of the latter's anti-religious views, but from 1922 Mussolini had been assiduously cultivating the support of the Church, introducing religious education in elementary schools, promoting Church secondary schools and increasing the salaries of bishops. He also held out the prospect of a settlement of the long-standing Church–state conflict. In return for these concessions, Pope Pius XI abandoned the Popolari, making no protest when its members were dropped from the government in April 1923 and forcing Sturzo, its leader, to resign in July 1923 and go into exile shortly afterwards. Mussolini had rescued the Bank of Rome, the largest Catholic bank, from financial collapse in 1922 and a section of the Popolari, the so-called clerico-Fascists, supported Mussolini in the Matteotti crisis.[9] Though Fascists aimed to destroy the Catholic peasant leagues and trade unions, the Vatican was much more fearful of communism than of Fascism. The left was in no position to successfully oppose Mussolini since the Socialists had split into two groups, reformists and revolutionaries, and a further division had been created with the formation of a Communist Party.

To achieve a Fascist majority in parliament Mussolini had to have the support of other parties to pass the Acerbo Law. It is difficult to see why these parties supported a law which was certain to undermine their existence. However, the Liberals, including prominent politicians such as Giolitti, Salandra and Vittorio Emanuele Orlando, were persuaded to vote for the bill for a variety of what appeared at the time to be good reasons. They believed it would facilitate the incorporation of Fascism into the political system, commit Mussolini to support of parliament and separate him from the radical members of his own party. On the other hand, they feared that if it was not passed Mussolini might be provoked into abolishing parliament altogether. They were impressed by the claim that the Acerbo Law would result in strong government, a powerful argument given the paralysis of previous administrations. The alternative to Mussolini was thought to be anarchy, and most Liberals feared social-ism and communism more than Fascism. Lastly, the more conservative Liberals were looking forward to being included in Mussolini's list for the next election, thus guaranteeing their seats.

The Popolari's attitude was also crucial; influenced by the Vatican, they decided by two votes to abstain, and in the event split, with only a few deputies voting against the bill. They too preferred Fascism to communism. The Democrats and some Socialists also abstained and only left-wing Socialists and Communists opposed the measure. Intimidation also played a part: Blackshirts roamed the Chamber and as one Fascist deputy said threateningly, 'you are more here inside, but we are more outside'.[10] The bill was eventually agreed by a large majority, with the result that 'an overwhelmingly non-Fascist parliament passed . . . a law putting an end to parliamentary government as hitherto known'.[11]

In the event, Mussolini did not need the Acerbo Law. In the April 1924 election, the Fascist list won 66 per cent of the votes and two-thirds of the seats. The election was portrayed as a triumph, but the Fascists had benefited from the electoral alliance with the Liberals, especially in southern Italy where Fascism had made little headway. They were also assisted by intimidation and corruption on an unprecedented scale. But it was also undoubtedly the case that for many of the voters Fascism proved more popular than its rivals. Mussolini was seen as the architect of effective government and was given some of the credit for the economic upturn which had succeeded the post-war crisis.

However, no sooner was the election over than Mussolini faced his most serious challenge. As a result of Matteotti's murder his popularity slumped. In June 1924 and again in November and December he was close to having to resign. That Mussolini survived the immediate crisis in June was due to the King's reluctance to dismiss him, a large vote of confidence in the Senate at the end of June, and the divisions and miscalculations of the opposition. Parliament was adjourned and while the Aventine secession had some initial impact, it quickly lost momentum.

It weakened the parliamentary opposition to Mussolini and gave the King an excuse for inactivity, especially since the Aventine deputies could not agree on what action to take: for example, they rejected a Communist proposal for a general strike, with the result that the Communists returned to parliament. In July the Pope forbade the already weakened Popolari to join the Socialists in an anti-Fascist front. When the Aventine secessionists tried to return to parliament in November 1925, they were refused entry. Leading Liberals such as Giolitti, possibly the only politician at the time with the authority to replace Mussolini, vacillated for several months before dissociating themselves from his government. Even when they finally did so, Mussolini continued to be supported by the King. Victor Emmanuel, mindful as ever of his own position, was full of trepidation at the consequences of removing Mussolini and could see no reason to dismiss him while he still had a parliamentary majority; in any case there appeared to be no available alternative government. The army, the only force capable of overthrowing Mussolini, had been partly conciliated by his moderating gestures in restraining the radicals in the Fascist Party and in obliging the militia in August 1924 to take an oath of loyalty to the King.

Mussolini's tactics, though often contradictory and vacillatory, also helped him to survive. He played for time, dismissing some Fascists and bringing right-wing Liberals and Nationalists into the government and veered between moderation and extremism, trying to reconcile all shades of opinion. Nevertheless, he was in a difficult position. The *ras* and the squads were prepared to turn against him if he continued to temporize. A Fascist rally in Florence at the end of December 1924 pronounced that loyalty to the Duce (Mussolini) was conditional on his taking 'dictatorial action'[12] and on 31 December a group of militia leaders descended on Mussolini to deliver a similar warning. Finally Mussolini acted. On 3 January he made what was arguably the most important speech of his career. In a statement described by one paper as 'the Caporetto of the old parliamentary liberalism',[13] he won back the initiative. He accepted responsibility for the events of the preceding months, dared the Chamber to impeach him and promised decisive action against opponents. Immediately Fascist squads moved in to crush opposition parties and close down newspapers. The Matteotti scandal petered out. Five Fascists were eventually put on trial for Matteotti's murder but two were acquitted and the other three, though sentenced to six years' imprisonment, were released after two months.

The opposition had let their chance slip and Mussolini was quick to take advantage, suppressing other political parties and censoring the press. The decree of December 1925 effectively destroyed parliamentary democracy, making Mussolini Head of Government, accountable only to the King.

Meanwhile Mussolini began to curb the Fascist Party. The structure of the Grand Council enabled him to exert control over the *ras*, while their absorption into a national militia partly neutralized the squads. In February 1925, he appointed Farinacci, previously one of the more revolutionary Fascists, as general secretary. Now 'poacher turned gamekeeper',[14] Farinacci zealously set about his task of imposing unity and discipline on the party. His role was to disempower the party, but no sooner had he achieved some success than he was replaced by Augusto Turati in March 1926. At the party conference in June 1925 criticism and discussion were banned. Party officials were increasingly appointed rather than elected and the local bosses lost much of their power.

Mussolini had surmounted the Matteotti crisis as much by good luck and the weakness of his opponents as by good management. But even during this crisis most Italians were prepared to give him the benefit of the doubt and he had had the advantage of support from industrialists who welcomed growing economic prosperity. Now organized in Confindustria (the Confederation of Industrialists), industrialists supported the economic policies of the Finance Minister, Alberto De Stefani, who had reduced taxes, limited government intervention in the economy, dropped investigations into war profits and abolished price and rent controls. They were also gratified by the fact that from 1925 only Fascist unions were allowed and, from April 1926, strikes were forbidden. Support for the regime was also forthcoming from respected intellectuals such as Pareto and Giovanni Gentile, a member of Mussolini's first cabinet. Many of the Italian public were apparently also prepared to turn a blind eye to Fascist violence and accept a dictatorship in preference to the previous instability.

## Questions

1. Analyse the stages by which the Fascists established and consolidated their control of Italy in the period 1922–6. How do you explain the failure of their opponents to resist them?
2. Why did democratic politicians and parties prove unable to prevent Mussolini from establishing a dictatorship between 1922 and 1926?

# SOURCES

## 1. THE MATTEOTTI CRISIS

### Source A: Mussolini's speech to the Fascist conference, August 1924.

We must chloroform ... the Opposition and the Italian people. The state of mind of the Italian people is this: do anything but let us know afterwards. Don't tell us every day that you want to bring in firing squads. That annoys us.

### Source B: Victor Emmanuel's view of the Matteotti crisis.

I am blind and deaf, my eyes and ears are the senate and the chamber of deputies.

### Source C: Mussolini's speech to the Chamber, 3 January 1925.

First of all there was the Aventine Secession, an unconstitutional secession that was clearly subversive *(lively approval)*. Then there followed a press campaign that lasted through June, July and August; a filthy, disgraceful campaign that dishonoured us for three months *(vigorous, prolonged applause)*. ... Very well, I now declare before this assembly and before the entire Italian people that I assume, I alone, political, moral and historical responsibility for all that has happened *(very vigorous and repeated applause. Many voices shouting, 'We are with you! All with you!')*. ... If Fascism has been nothing more than castor oil and the truncheon, instead of being a proud passion of the best part of Italian youth, then I am to blame *(applause)*. If Fascism has been a criminal association, then I am the chief of this criminal association! *(vigorous applause)* ... If all the violence has been the result of a particular historical, political and moral climate, then responsibility for this is mine, because I have created this climate with a propaganda that has lasted from the Intervention Crisis until today.

Gentlemen, Italy wants peace, tranquillity, calm in which to work. We shall give her this tranquillity by means of love if possible but by force if necessary *(lively applause)*.

You may be sure that within twenty-four hours after this speech, the situation will be clarified in its every aspect.

### Source D: Mussolini describes the Matteotti crisis in *My Autobiography* (London, 1938: first published in Italy 1928).

One day Matteotti disappeared from Rome. Immediately it was whispered that a political crime had been committed. The Socialists were looking for a martyr who might be of use for their oratory, and at once, before anything definite could possibly be known, they accused Fascism. By my orders we began the most anxious and complex investigations. The Government decided to act with the greatest energy, not only for reasons of justice, but also to stop, from the first moment, the spreading of any kind of calumny. . . . Very soon it was possible to find the guilty. . . . They came from the Fascist group, but they were completely outside our responsible elements.

The sternest proceedings were taken against them without limit or reservation.

. . .

All this should have stilled the storm.

### Source E: Mussolini recalls the Matteotti crisis in 1944 (this was written by Mussolini in the Republic of Salò after his removal from power).

1924 . . . was a most critical year. The Regime had to face the consequences of a crime which, apart from any other consideration, was a political error both in method and timing.

In the summer of 1924 the pressure of the Aventine group on the King and his immediate entourage was very strong. . . . The King had given certain general assurances as far as legal punishment of the crime was concerned, but hesitated in following the men of the Aventine into the domain of political responsibility.

Even Cesare Rossi's famous memorandum of the end of December (published on the Government's initiative, so as to anticipate their opponents) did not make much impression on the King. The opponents of Fascism were henceforth bottled up in a moral question with no way out; and also, by going into exile, they had cleared the ground – that ground on which a counter-attack was to be launched at the right moment by the Regime.

### Questions

1. Explain the references to the Aventine secession and the intervention crisis (Source C). [4]
2. What do Sources A, B and E reveal of the reasons why Mussolini was able to stay in power between June and December 1924? [5]
3. In what ways could the Matteotti murder be described as 'a political error both in method and timing' (Source E)? [4]
*4. Examine the ways in which the language and content of Mussolini's speech in Source C are designed to win the support of his audience. [5]
5. How reliable as evidence for the historian are Mussolini's accounts of the Matteotti crisis in Sources D and E? [7]

**Worked answer**

*4. [Note that this answer requires analysis of the style – that is use of language and expression – as well as the content of the speech.]*

Oratory was one of Mussolini's strengths but this was still a difficult speech. Mussolini probably anticipated few problems in the Chamber, which was overwhelmingly Fascist, but he was appealing not just to parliament but to the public at large. On 3 January many of his opponents were confident that he would have to resign and therefore a number of interest groups outside parliament had to be convinced of his ability to surmount the crisis.

Mussolini was careful to use language likely to appeal to his parliamentary and wider audiences, for example in references to love of Italy and to the intervention crisis (reminding Italians of his patriotic and nationalist credentials) and in phrases such as 'proud passion', and by invoking 'Italian youth'. The appeal to 'peace, tranquillity, calm' would particularly strike a chord with many Italians who were growing tired of the upheaval of the previous few months and desired nothing more than the stability promised by Mussolini. He also did not hesitate to brand opposition as 'subversive' and the press campaign as 'filthy' and 'disgraceful'.

The content of the speech was also important. Mussolini avoided mention of Matteotti, while presenting himself as a strong figure who was prepared to take responsibility for his actions (an implicit contrast with the irresoluteness of previous governments). He counterposed the less attractive side of Fascism, 'castor oil' and 'truncheons', with its positive aspects, the appeal to youth and national pride. But there was also the threat of force and promise of speedy action: these would convince Italians that he would prevail and had put the crisis behind him, while making opponents much less certain of success.

# SOURCES

## 2. THE ESTABLISHMENT OF A DICTATORSHIP

### Source F: Law on the powers of the Head of Government, December 1925.

1. The executive power is exercised by His Majesty the King through his government...
2. The Prime Minister is Head of Government.
3. The Head of Government... is appointed and recalled by the King...

4. The Head of Government . . . directs and co-ordinates the activities of the Ministers . . .
5. No bill or motion may be submitted to either of the Houses of Parliament without the consent of the Head of Government.

### Source G: Law for the Defence of the State, November 1926.

Whoever reconstitutes . . . any association, organization, or party that has been dissolved by order of the public authority, is liable to imprisonment ranging from three to ten years. . . .

Whoever is a member of such associations . . . is liable . . . to imprisonment ranging from two to five years. . . .

The crimes referred to in this law shall be brought before a Special Tribunal, to consist of a president chosen from among the general officers of the Royal Army, the Royal Navy, the Royal Air Force and the Voluntary Militia for National Security. . . . The formation of this tribunal is to be ordered by the Minister of War, who will determine its composition.

### Source H: Mussolini's circular to the prefects, January 1927.

I solemnly affirm that the prefect is the highest authority of the state in the province. He is the direct representative of the central executive power. . . . Whenever necessary, the prefect must stimulate and harmonize the various activities of the party. . . . The party and its members, from the highest to the lowest, now that the revolution is complete, are only a conscious instrument of the will of the state. . . . Now that the state is equipped with all its own methods of prevention and repression there are some 'residues' that must disappear. I am speaking of '*squadrismo*' which in 1927 is simply anachronistic, sporadic, but which reappears in an undisciplined fashion during periods of public commotion. These illegal activities must stop . . . the era of reprisals, destruction and violence is over.

### Source I: A German visitor, Count Kessler, comments on Mussolini's position in March 1927.

Mussolini's position is entirely secure . . . Mussolini . . . does now represent Italy and anyone who wants to be on terms with Italy must come to terms with Mussolini.

### Questions

1. Identify the 'prefects' and the 'party' (Source H). [4]
*2. How extensive were the powers accorded to Mussolini in Sources F and H? [4]
3. How would the provisions in Source G reduce the likelihood of opposition to Mussolini's regime? [4]

4. Why was Mussolini eager to restrain the activities of *squadrismo* in 1927 (Source H)? [5]
5. Using all the Sources and your own knowledge, how far do you agree with the assertion in Source I that 'Mussolini's position is entirely secure'? [8]

### Worked answer

*2. Mussolini acquired considerable powers by the law of December 1925. His new role as Head of Government conferred greater authority than he had held as Prime Minister and made him irremovable except by the King. As indicated in article 4, he had supremacy over the other ministers in the government who were dependent on his approval. He also decided which matters could be discussed in parliament, though as this was almost entirely Fascist at this time, it was unlikely to oppose him.

In Source H he affirms the role of the prefects, who had replaced elected local government. As Mussolini states, they are the representatives of the government. In addition they were all appointed by Mussolini. This gave him extra powers over local government and also, equally importantly, over the Fascist Party since the prefects are being given the role of harmonizing party activities; Mussolini goes on to instruct them to discipline the squads, whose 'illegal activities must stop'.

However, Mussolini was still not wholly supreme since he had to share some powers with the King who in theory had the power to remove him.

# 4

# A TOTALITARIAN REGIME?

## Mussolini and the Fascist state

### BACKGROUND NARRATIVE

By the end of 1926 Mussolini was ready to put the finishing touches
to his dictatorship. A law of 1928 abolished universal suffrage and cut
the electorate by two-thirds; henceforth the franchise depended
on payment of 100 lire in tax or membership of a Fascist syndicate.
Votes in any case did not count for very much since Italy was now
a one-party state and the Fascist Grand Council selected the 400
members of the Chamber of Deputies. Not surprisingly, the March
1929 plebiscite saw a 90 per cent vote in favour of the Fascist list
and there was a similar majority for the regime in the referendum
of 1934. In 1939 a Chamber of Fasces and Corporations, reflecting
the development of the corporate state, replaced the Chamber of
Deputies.

Mussolini himself monopolized as many state offices as possible.
For much of the period from 1926 he held between seven and nine
portfolios (government departments), including the Ministry of the
Interior which gave him control over the police and local government,
and the Foreign and Defence ministries. He could not possibly run
all these departments effectively and decision-making was often arbi-
trary and chaotic as a result. Though reasonably industrious, the Duce
did not work very long hours, but often left the light on in his office
at night to give the impression of continuous toil.

To sustain popularity, the regime relied heavily on propaganda, which was taken very seriously and orchestrated by the Ministry for Press and Propaganda and, from 1937, the Ministry of Popular Culture. The greatest effort was devoted to promoting the cult of the Duce. Mussolini was in reality a vain and solitary individual, but he wanted to be seen as strong and decisive, a man of action. Within Italy he acquired an almost godlike status and was variously portrayed as the 'new Caesar', as a great statesman and military leader, as a vigorous athlete, or in a populist pose helping peasants with the harvest. Italians were bombarded with slogans such as 'Mussolini is always right'[1] and 'believe, obey, fight'. Mussolini himself commented: 'often I would like to be wrong but so far it has never happened and events have always turned out just as I foresaw.'[2] After coming to power he liked to present himself as a family man, devoted to his wife Rachele (whom he belatedly married in a Church ceremony to placate the Vatican) and his five children, but in fact he was rarely at home, preferring to spend his time with a series of mistresses, the last of whom, Clara Petacci, shared his fate.

As well as extolling Mussolini's virtues, propaganda emphasized the regime's links with the ancient Roman Empire, utilizing symbols such as the *fasces* (claimed to have originated from the rods carried by Roman magistrates), the wolf and eagle, and the Roman salute. The march on Rome was said to have inaugurated an Italian rebirth, symbolized by a new calendar dating from Year 1 in 1922. New holidays were introduced, such as 21 April to celebrate the founding of Rome, and special exhibitions were mounted, for example in 1932 to mark the tenth anniversary of the march on Rome, and in 1937 to celebrate the 2,000th anniversary of the birth of the Roman Emperor Augustus. Public enthusiasm was sustained by a round of speeches, ceremonies and parades.

Mussolini never lost his flair for publicity. He could be an inspiring orator and enjoyed haranguing the crowds from the balcony of Palazzo Venezia where he had his office. In reality he was contemptuous of the masses, whom he said were 'stupid, dirty, do not work hard enough and are content with their little cinema shows'.[3] He also took a keen interest in journalism, resuming the editorship of his newspaper, *Popolo d'Italia*, after his brother Arnaldo's death in 1931. The press was the main vehicle for propaganda but Mussolini also sought to exploit the newer forms of media such as radio and cinema. The first radio stations had been set up in 1925, and while radio ownership was lower than in most other European countries, large numbers of Italians were able to listen to Mussolini's speeches broadcast in town squares and other public places. Some radio programmes were specifically designed to promote the regime, for example 'The Balilla's Friend',[4] a popular nightly series for children, though most had a purely entertainment function. The cinema was also popular. The Istituto Nazionale LUCE was set up in 1924 to produce documentary films extolling the successes of the regime, such as the draining of the Pontine Marshes and the Abyssinian campaign. From April 1926, all cinemas had to show official newsreels. However, the few propaganda feature films which were made were not very convincing.

One of Mussolini's greatest coups was the signing of the Lateran Pacts with the Vatican. Though privately Mussolini remained an anti-clerical atheist, he was quick to perceive the political advantages of a settlement with the Church. Negotiations to resolve the long-standing Church–state dispute predated his regime but from 1922 the pace increased and the Pacts were finally signed in February 1929.

There were three parts to the Pacts: a treaty about sovereignty, a Concordat dealing with Church–state relations and a financial settlement. At first sight the Papacy appeared to have benefited the most. The Pope was confirmed as head of a sovereign state, the Vatican City, he received compensation for loss of territory and Catholicism was to be the sole religion of the Italian state. The Vatican continued to appoint the bishops while the state paid the clergy. There was to be compulsory religious instruction in state schools, and Church schools gained parity with their state counterparts. Civil marriage was no longer a legal requirement. In return the Church recognized the Italian state.

However, Mussolini arguably gained just as much from the Pacts as the Vatican. They greatly improved his standing in Italy, especially among the more religious sections of the population, and he also won international acclaim for a settlement which had eluded all previous Italian governments. Also, the Pacts presumed that the Church would support the Fascist regime. There was in fact considerable common ground between Catholicism and Fascism, which had paved the way for the compromise. Both were implacably opposed to communism and socialism, and both agreed on social issues such as the role of women and the desirability of a high birth rate. Pope Pius XI went so far as to describe Mussolini as a 'man sent by Providence'.[5] However, Church–state relations were never completely harmonious and they deteriorated in the 1930s. The main point of friction was the government's attempts to close down Catholic Action's youth organizations, which competed with the Fascist youth movement, the Balilla. In June 1931, the Pope protested, issuing an encyclical, *Non abbiamo bisogno*, which challenged the Fascist monopoly of educational activities. In September 1931 a compromise was reached whereby Catholic Action was restricted to religious and educational functions, though its youth organization was permitted to continue with a circumscribed role. However, the German alliance, the adoption of racial policies in 1938 and entry into the war were to further antagonize the Church.

## ANALYSIS (1): HOW FAR IS IT CORRECT TO DESCRIBE MUSSOLINI AS A 'WEAK DICTATOR'?

In many respects Mussolini was a strong dictator. His role as Head of Government gave him considerable powers, greatly exceeding those of a Prime Minister. Italy was a one-party state where all laws were made by the Duce. Parliament was disregarded and only met to applaud Mussolini's speeches. There was no such thing as collective cabinet responsibility; as well as appropriating several cabinet posts for himself, Mussolini preferred to have individual meetings with the other ministers – who were often nonentities – the better to manipulate them, and he made frequent ministerial changes. He also appointed the prefects and other local government officials. In theory the Grand Council could decide the succession to both Mussolini and the King, but it was never in a position to use these powers. Mussolini rarely summoned it and it was not consulted at all on most important issues. Mussolini's power was also boosted by propaganda and a personality cult, which portrayed him as an invincible leader.

But despite all this, Mussolini did not achieve the complete control to which he aspired. He depended on keeping the support of the conservative forces which had assisted his rise to power, particularly the landed and business elites, the army and the Church. Equally important, unlike Germany where Hitler was supreme after the death of President Hindenburg, Italy still had a monarch as Head of State. Mussolini was obliged to coexist with Victor Emmanuel who in theory had the power to dismiss him. Though the King was unlikely to use this prerogative as long as the regime was successful and popular, he nevertheless posed a potential threat to Mussolini's position. Also, the armed forces swore an oath of loyalty to the King, not the Duce. In addition, Victor Emmanuel appointed the Senate and, though this body was highly conservative, its life members were independent of Mussolini and were not above occasionally criticizing him. Because of these constraints on his authority, Mussolini would have liked to abolish the monarchy, but he was never in a strong enough position to attempt this.

Mussolini also had to contend with the Church, which remained an alternative focus of loyalty for many Italians. The Lateran Pacts had strengthened the Vatican's position and, though they also tied it to the Fascist regime, its support was conditional. The Church was wary of the claims made by some Fascists to be creating a new religion and morality, and the disagreements over Catholic Action and the German alliance led to it becoming increasingly dissociated from the regime.

Most Italian institutions were only marginally influenced by Fascism and experienced little change of personnel or outlook. The armed forces (except for the airforce, which was new) successfully resisted Fascist infiltration and the Fascist militia, unlike the SS in Germany, was only allowed a minor role. There was no wholesale purge of the civil service, though all public employees were obliged to join the Fascist Party. The main changes were in the judiciary where some judges were removed, but in general the old ruling class survived intact. Even the mafia, which Mussolini claimed to have eliminated, merely went underground to resurface in Sicily on the side of the Allies towards the end of the war.

Mussolini was more successful in subduing the Fascist Party. Article 1 of the party charter of 1932 accurately described the party as 'a civilian militia at the orders of the Duce and in the service of the Fascist state'.[6] Among Mussolini's supporters there had always been tension between revolutionary syndicalists on the one hand and nationalists and conservatives on the other, but Mussolini was primarily concerned to maintain the confidence of the latter groups. Once he had consolidated his position, the activity of some party members and of the squads, who went on the rampage in Florence in October 1925, became an embarrassment. Mussolini had needed the party to get to power but there was to be no party take-over of the state.

Mussolini curbed the party by playing off its numerous competing factions, appointing compliant general secretaries (Turati from 1926 and Achille Starace from 1932 to 1939) and local leaders, and exploiting the turnover in its membership. From 300,000 in 1921, party membership rose to 1.5 million in 1933, 2.5 million in 1939 and 5 million in 1943.[7] But many old and founder members had been purged in the mid-1920s and the influx of new recruits, mostly white-collar and public employees, helped to make the party docile and depoliticized it since most joined not out of conviction but in order to keep their jobs or further their careers. Fascism had developed 'middle-aged spread'.[8]

Locally, the prefects were more powerful than the party bosses. Several of the most potentially troublesome *ras* were 'promoted' to prestigious but out-of-the-way posts, Grandi as ambassador to London, and Balbo to Libya. No party secret police force was created, as happened in Germany, and the state police, under the control of Arturo Bocchini from 1927 to 1940, remained firmly independent of the party.

The PNF did gain some new spheres of influence in running organizations such as the Dopolavoro ('after work') and the Balilla (the youth movement), and in relief work among the poor, children and war veterans; but though the burgeoning party bureaucracy employed increasing numbers of officials, it was barred from any influence over policy. 'The party and the Militia tended increasingly to become ceremonial leftovers from the days of the "Revolution".'[9] As Blinkhorn points out, 'Fascist Italy may have been a one-party state, but it was not a "party-state" such as Soviet Russia or even Nazi Germany.'[10]

Mussolini was by no means a 'weak dictator', but the relative ease with which he was eventually removed in July 1943 illustrates the limitations of his authority. In the last resort, his rule depended on consensus and continued success and, when public support evaporated, both the Grand Council and King retained enough power to depose him.

## Questions

1. To what extent was Mussolini obliged to share power with established groups or institutions after 1925?
2. What were the advantages and disadvantages to Mussolini of his agreements with the Church in 1929?

## ANALYSIS (2): WHY WAS THERE SO LITTLE OPPOSITION TO MUSSOLINI WITHIN ITALY AND TO WHAT EXTENT DID ITALIANS SUPPORT THE FASCIST REGIME?

The attitudes of Italians towards Mussolini's regime are difficult to assess. There was no opportunity to express a free choice in elections and press censorship ensured that there was almost no public criticism. The large 'yes' votes in the 1929 and 1934 plebiscites are misleading since there were no choices on offer and abstentions and 'no' votes attracted unwelcome attention. Active opposition scarcely existed, but this did not necessarily mean that the regime was enthusiastically supported since dissent could only be expressed in oblique form; as Galeazzo Ciano noted in 1938, 'there are still three kinds of anti-Fascist demonstrations in Italy, funerals, the theatre and witticisms'.[11] The ambivalence of these attitudes is captured in the comments of an Italian officer in 1943: 'the real truth is this: there were very few anti-Fascists in Italy. To curse about Fascist dress, to tell jokes; that was not anti-Fascism. It was moral confusion.'[12] But even Mussolini ruefully concluded that 'consent is as unstable as the sand formations on the edge of the sea'.[13]

The lack of overt opposition to the Fascist regime can be explained by a combination of factors, namely repression, propaganda and the fact that most Italians, at any rate up to the outbreak of the Second World War, were not greatly dissatisfied. Mussolini was certainly determined to suppress opponents. Non-Fascist parties and independent unions were banned and the 1926 Law for the Defence of the State set up special military tribunals to try political crimes, with no jury or appeal. In 1927 a secret police, the OVRA, with a network of informers, was established. But this said, repression, certainly by the standards of Nazi Germany, was relatively mild. The OVRA was not a party organization and 'was little more than a slightly better organization of the political section that had always existed within the traditional police'.[14] There were no concentration camps, fewer than 5,000 political prisoners and only nine people were executed for political offences between 1927 and 1940. The usual punishments were exile abroad or to remote parts of southern Italy or the Italian islands. The regime even tolerated some limited dissent; for example, the historian Benedetto Croce was allowed to remain in Italy and to criticize Mussolini though other leading figures such as the historian, Gaetano Salvemini, and the musical director, Arturo Toscanini, were forced into exile.

Mussolini had stated that 'to govern . . . you need only two things, policemen and bands playing in the streets':[15] Fascist Italy relied more on bands than on policemen. Thanks to a personality cult Mussolini generally remained quite popular. Successes in sports and athletics were attributed to Fascism and widely celebrated. Pressure was put on newspaper owners, editors and foreign correspondents to ensure favourable reporting, both at home and abroad. The September 1928 Press Office code of conduct declared that 'news of air and rail disasters and bank failures was to be restricted and even natural catastrophes were to be treated "with great sobriety"',[16] while apparent successes such as the building of new highways and land settlement schemes were played up. The radio was a means whereby Mussolini's speeches could reach large audiences, while exploits such as the Abyssinian campaign were publicized in the newsreels shown with every cinema performance.

Conformism was also ensured by participation in the activities of the Balilla, the Fascist youth movement, and the Dopolavoro, the after work organization, as well as by the requirement that employees in most professions had to join Fascist syndicates. The Church's endorsement of the regime persuaded most Catholics to go along with it, though when the Vatican began to distance itself from Mussolini after 1938, the attitudes of most Catholics also changed accordingly. As discussed in chapter 5, though the majority of the urban and rural working class did not do particularly well out of Fascism, they were not sufficiently discontented to mount any more than the occasional sporadic protest.

Opposition to Mussolini within Italy was ineffective. The leaders of the Popolari, Socialists and Communists (Sturzo, Turati and Palmiro Togliatti) had fled the country and most of those opposition leaders who stayed behind, such as the socialist theorist Gramsci, were imprisoned. The Communists and Socialists set up organizations in exile, but apart from a few Communist factory cells in northern industrial areas, they had little success inside Italy before 1943. There was some anti-Fascism in the German- and Slav-speaking regions but this was largely a reaction to the Italianization policy followed in these areas. The only important Catholic anti-Fascist organization was the Movimento Guelfo d'Azione set up in Milan in 1928, but it was broken up in 1933 and its leaders arrested.

Mussolini's opponents faced the problem that the anti-Fascist parties were historically suspicious of one another and therefore reluctant to cooperate. An exception was Giustizia e Libertà, founded in 1929 by the Rosselli brothers, which tried to unite socialists, republicans and democrats, but it never acquired more than a few thousand supporters. Another obstacle was lack of support outside Italy (except minimally from France and Russia) and therefore shortage of funds.

But absence of opposition did not necessarily mean that all Italians genuinely supported the regime or were convinced by its propaganda. Fascism's appeal, based on strong leadership, order, loyalty and patriotism, undoubtedly struck a chord in a population which had learnt to identify democracy with failure. Most Italians applauded Mussolini's early foreign policy successes and especially the conquest of Abyssinia. However, propaganda was most successful when it went with the grain and reinforced existing attitudes. The more novel aims of 'remaking' Italians and creating a new warlike race did not have so much appeal; nor did the German alliance or the racial policies adopted after 1938. Fascist ideology failed to percolate very far and the National Fascist Institute of Culture set up by the PNF in 1925 to disseminate Fascist ideas to the masses was not successful.

There were significant class and regional variations in support for Fascism. Propaganda did not reach many rural areas where illiteracy was still high and the population had limited access to radio or cinema. It was particularly hard to disseminate Fascist ideology in southern Italy where there were strong regional traditions and suspicion of centralized state interference. The poorer classes, who were the most adversely affected by the depression and economic policies, seem to have been less receptive to Fascism than the middle and upper classes. In some industrial areas there were even occasional spontaneous protests at wage cuts, the reduction of the working week, and inadequate relief payments, some backed by Fascist unions (a phenomenon unheard of in Nazi Germany). As against this, some workers seem to have welcomed the recreational activities provided by the Dopolavoro and benefited from the improvements in education and the social services. But it was, paradoxically, the fact that Fascism did not succeed in intruding into most areas of life which did most to facilitate consensus.

Any analysis of Italian attitudes to Mussolini's regime also has to take into account the fluctuations in its popularity over the period from 1922 to 1943. Support was low in 1924 at the height of the Matteotti crisis, high in 1929 due to the agreement with the Church, lower in the depression of the early 1930s, at an all-time peak in 1936 during the Abyssinian war, reduced in the late 1930s due to the unpopularity of the German alliance, much diminished as a result of wartime defeats, and almost non-existent by 1943.[17]

It was indeed after entry into the war that disillusionment really surfaced, especially among industrial workers affected by rationing, shortages and rising prices, as well as among businesses hit by the decline in trade. Italians did not appear to be taken in by anti-British propaganda and most of them disliked subservience to Germany. The increase in industrial unrest, for example the well-supported strikes in March 1943, together with the rise of left-dominated resistance by partisans in German-occupied Italy, indicates that socialist and communist views might have been driven underground but had not been eradicated.

Most historians agree that there was no overwhelming enthusiasm for Fascism and concur that 'Italians did not internalize Fascist values'.[18] The great majority conformed as long as the regime was reasonably successful. But when Mussolini ran out of luck and fell from power in July 1943, few regretted his passing, an indication that support for Fascism had probably only ever been superficial.

## Questions

1. Why did opponents of Mussolini's Fascist regime meet with so little success?
2. To what extent was Fascism supported by the Italian public?
3. How effective was propaganda in mobilizing support for Mussolini and his regime?

## ANALYSIS (3): HOW SUCCESSFUL WERE MUSSOLINI AND HIS SUPPORTERS IN DEVELOPING A COHERENT FASCIST IDEOLOGY?

Before coming to power Mussolini possessed only the sketchiest of ideologies. One reason for this was that his views had swung in a short period of time from extreme left to extreme right, and were still to some extent unresolved in 1922. Another was that the Fascist movement was a mixture of factions and contradictory beliefs, with a membership ranging from former Socialists and syndicalists to futurists, interventionists and nationalists. To achieve power, Mussolini had needed to appear both conservative and revolutionary and after 1922 Fascists continued to be divided, some aiming to replace the old order with a new ruling class whereas others wished to preserve the social status quo.

Also, early Fascism had been characterized by negative attitudes rather than positive ones. As the Fascist leader Giuseppe Bottai remarked, 'you cannot talk philosophy with the enemy at the gates'.[19] Therefore there was no ready-made ideology in 1922, apart from advocacy of strong authoritarian government and nationalism. Otherwise, it was not clear what Fascism stood for beyond the acquisition of power or where it might go once power had been achieved. Not till after 1925, when he had consolidated his position, did Mussolini feel the need to develop a more substantial ideological base.

Ideology emerged in a piecemeal fashion and owed more to the nationalists than to the founders of the Fascist movement. First, Fascism came to be identified with totalitarianism. This concept was the major contribution to Fascist thought and was developed by the political philosopher Giovanni Gentile, the Minister for Education. In March 1925 he convened a congress of 200 intellectuals which produced a Fascist Manifesto. The first draft was insufficiently coherent but Gentile was not deterred and from 1925 to 1932 worked on the *Enciclopedia italiana*, contributing the article 'The Doctrine of Fascism', much of which was then revised by Mussolini. The latter had first described the Fascist regime as totalitarian in 1925 and the 'Doctrine of Fascism' expanded on this theme, asserting the primacy of the all-powerful state over its citizens. This clearly differentiated Fascism from liberalism, which emphasized the rights of the individual. The 'Doctrine' stated 'the Fascist conception of life stresses the importance of the state and accepts the individual only insofar as his interests coincide with those of the state . . . Fascism is totalitarian.'[20] Here Mussolini was asserting that the state should control all aspects of economic and social life.

However, while totalitarianism appeared to define Fascism and to set it apart from other systems of political thought, the practice fell far short of the theory. As we have seen, Mussolini was unable to subordinate many established interest groups and his rule was not in practice 'totalitarian'. He described himself as 'the most disobeyed dictator in history'.[21] Nor, as discussed in chapter 5, did Fascism come near to transforming Italian society in its own mould. Pollard's view is that totalitarianism can be considered as not much more than 'a rationalization of the dictatorship'.[22]

Along with totalitarianism went attempts to present Fascism as a total belief system. 'The Doctrine of Fascism' asserted that 'Fascism is a religious concept', and claimed that 'Fascism as well as being a system of government, is also and above all a system of thought.'[23] The suggestion that Fascism might be a religion was certain to bring Mussolini into conflict with the Church, so he was obliged to qualify it by adding, 'the state does not have a theology but it does have a morality.'[24]

The second theoretical contribution to Fascism was the concept of the corporate state, the work of the Nationalist, Alfredo Rocco, Minister of Justice from 1926 to 1932 and of Bottai, a former futurist who was Minister of Corporations from 1929 to 1932. The idea of corporations derived partly from early twentieth-century syndicalism with its emphasis on the economic unit as the basis of society, and partly from the medieval guilds to which all producers in a particular area of work had belonged. Corporations could be seen as an alternative to both capitalism and communism. The aim was to combine workers and employers in the same organizations, each covering a section of the economy, which would regulate production and guarantee good industrial relations. Implementation began with the Chigi Palace Pact of December 1923 and the Vidoni Palace Pact of October 1925, signed between the Confederation of Industry and the Fascist Labour Confederation. In July 1926 a Ministry of Corporations was established and in 1930 a National Council of Corporations. Finally, in 1934, twenty-two corporations were set up for the various branches of economic activity. Mussolini intended that corporations should become the basis of the political system, but this experiment did not begin till 1939 and was disrupted by the war.

In an article in *Popolo d'Italia* in 1934 Mussolini extolled corporatism in typically exalted but fairly meaningless terms as 'an integrated, unified vision of life and of man which influences every human activity, individual and collective'.[25] Some of the more radical Fascists took corporatism seriously as a means to improve the lot of the working class. But, as with totalitarianism, little changed in practice. Class relationships were not altered, employers' interests predominated and Fascist unions' bargaining power proved negligible. The corporate state turned out to be 'an artificial veneer on an essentially unprincipled movement'.[26]

Third, from 1938, racial and anti-Semitic theories were grafted onto the existing ideology. In the Manifesto of Racialist Scientists in July 1938, it was asserted that 'the people of present-day Italy are of Aryan origin and their civilization is Aryan. . . . A pure Italian race is already in existence. . . . The Jews do not belong to the Italian race'.[27] In autumn 1938, laws similar to the 1935 Nuremberg Laws in Germany were enacted, prohibiting mixed marriages, banning Jewish children from schools and Jews from public employment and ownership of businesses or property. In practice one-fifth of Jews were exempt on the grounds of having served in the army or the civil service, but the legislation bore heavily on the rest.

Various explanations have been put forward to account for these racial views which were the more surprising since there were only about 50,000 well-integrated Jews in Italy and little overt anti-Semitism prior to 1938. One explanation is that it was another opportunistic move, introduced to 'catch up with Germany' and cement the Axis alliance. However, Fascism had always contained an element of racism, exemplified by *romanità*, the belief that Italians were descended from the ancient Romans. Anti-Semitic attitudes were not new and had long been accepted by the Church, though the Vatican opposed the racial laws. The Abyssinian war, which greatly intensified imperialism, may have been another factor. Mussolini himself specifically related the racial theories and laws to the Italian conquest of empire.

Finally, in 1943, Mussolini made a final ideological shift when, set up by the Germans in the Republic of Salò, he returned to some of the more anti-capitalist ideas he had espoused in the early days of his movement.

Fascism's claims to have produced an ideology rested largely on the concepts of totalitarianism and the corporate state. But not only were these ideas developed some time after Mussolini came to power; in addition, neither could they effectively be put into practice. Furthermore, a good deal of Fascist theorizing was vague, woolly and obscure, as exemplified by the School of Fascist Mysticism set up in Milan in 1930. Though most Italian intellectuals went along with Fascism, intellectual coherence was lacking. Most historians take the view that Mussolini was interested in ideology only to the extent that it bolstered his own position. They see him as an opportunist and essentially pragmatic politician intent on gaining and keeping power as an end in itself, and they see his regime as a personal rather than an ideological dictatorship.[28] As Cassels points out, Fascism may have amounted to not much more than 'Mussolinism'.[29]

## Questions

1. To what extent did Italian Fascism succeed in acquiring a coherent and consistent ideology?
2. Why and with what results did the Fascist regime introduce racist legislation in the late 1930s?

# SOURCES

## 1. PROPAGANDA AND PUBLIC OPINION

### Source A: See Plate 1.

[See illustration on page 58]

### Source B: See Plate 2.

[See illustration on page 59]

### Source C: A police report on opposition in Ancona, a town in north-central Italy, in 1937.

At Jesi up until now Fascist penetration has been relatively ineffectual. On the other hand, we have only thirteen subversives on file, and they are constantly under surveillance. A few copies of anti-Fascist newspapers have come in (sent by unknown persons to the *podestà* or to a handful of private individuals of impeccable conduct). In September of last year some anti-Fascist leaflets were found in the office of the match factory.

### Source D: Factory workers and Fascism.

A high Fascist official visited a factory and asked the manager: 'What are these workers' politics?' 'One third communist, one third socialist, and the rest belong to small parties,' was the reply. 'What!' cried the livid Fascist: 'Is none of them Fascist?' The manager hastened to reassure him: 'All of them, your Excellency, all of them.'

CREDERE    OBBEDIRE
           COMBATTERE

*Plate 1   Il Duce*, Mussolini, in military uniform, gives a speech from a
rostrum containing a typical Fascist slogan: 'Believe', 'obey', 'fight'.
© Peter Newark's Military Pictures

*Plate 2*  Mussolini encouraging the harvesters at Aprilla. © Popperfoto

**Source E: Peasant attitudes to Fascism in the mid-1930s quoted from Carlo Levi, *Christ Stopped at Eboli* (first published in Italy in 1945), a description of a remote part of southern Italy where the author was exiled for opposing the regime.**

None of the peasants were members [of the Fascist Party]; indeed it was unlikely that they should belong to any party.... Such matters had nothing to do with them. ... What had the peasants to do with Power, Government and the State?... The third of October [1935], which marked the official opening of the [Abyssinian] war, was a miserable sort of day. Twenty or twenty-five peasants roped in by the *carabinieri* and the Fascist Scouts stood woodenly in the square to listen to the historic pronouncement that came over the radio ... the war so lightheartedly set in motion from Rome was greeted in Gafliano with stony indifference. Mayor Don Luigi spoke from the balcony of the town hall. He enlarged on the eternal grandeur of Rome, the seven hills, the wolf that suckled Romulus and Remus, Caesar's legions, Roman civilization and the Roman Empire which was about to be revived. ... Huddled against the wall below, the peasants listened in silence, shielding their eyes with their hands from the sun and looking as dark and gloomy as bats in their black suits.

## Questions

1. Explain the slogan on the rostrum in the photograph of Mussolini in Source A. [2]
*2. In what sense can the photographs of Mussolini in Source A and Source B be regarded as propaganda? [5]
3. How do Sources B and E differ in their portrayal of the attitudes of the peasants to Fascism? [5]
4  What do Sources C and D reveal about the attitude of industrial workers to the Fascist regime? [5]
5. Using all the Sources and your own knowledge, assess the effectiveness of propaganda in Fascist Italy. [8]

## Worked answer

* 2. Both these illustrations are propaganda designed to promote the cult of the Duce and to present Mussolini in different impressive poses. In Source A he is depicted as a strong, imposing military leader, surrounded by commanders of the armed forces; his role is emphasized by the slogan. The severe backdrop of granite pillars and the height of the rostrum accentuate the imposing setting. Mussolini is pictured as invincible and so is Italy's military might, as illustrated by the stack of rifles and banners. This image was misleading, since Mussolini did not

in fact possess most of the qualities ascribed to him, nor were Italy's armed forces so powerful as suggested.

Source B portrays Mussolini in a quite different role. Here he is seen as a man of the people, identifying with the peasants who are looking on admiringly. This illustration attempts to show Mussolini as concerned to promote the well-being of the humblest citizen, through the 'Battle for Grain', a government campaign to increase wheat production. This again is inaccurate propaganda; Mussolini in fact had contempt for most of the Italian population. Also, as Source E shows, the reality was that many peasants were indifferent to Mussolini and to the achievements of Fascism.

# SOURCES

## 2. MUSSOLINI'S RELATIONS WITH THE CHURCH

### Source F: Extracts from the Lateran Pacts, February 1929.

Art. 1 ... the Roman Catholic and Apostolic Religion is the sole religion of the State.
Art. 20 Bishops before taking possession of their dioceses shall take an oath of loyalty at the hands of the Head of State....
Art. 36 ... the religious instruction now given in the public elementary school shall be further developed in the secondary schools....
Art. 43 The Italian State recognizes the auxiliary organizations of the 'Azione Cattolica Italiana' [Catholic Action] inasmuch as these ... carry on their activities independently of all political parties and under the immediate direction of the Hierarchy of the Church for the teaching and practice of Catholic principles.

### Source G: *The Times* (12 February 1929) comments on the Church–state agreement.

The resolution of the Roman question was the result ... of a bold stroke of statesmanship. The prestige of the Head of Government must be greatly increased in Italy and abroad ... Italy's prestige will ... be greatly strengthened by the cessation of the quarrel with the pope.

### Source H: The American magazine *Time* describes the role of the Church in the 1929 plebiscite.

Leaning forward in a carved armchair at the Palazzo Chigi, Signor Benito Mussolini sat with his hard chin cupped between contented palms watching newsreel flashes of Cardinals and Monsignors marching to the ballot box, attended by blaring brass bands and wildly cheering throngs. Never before have Princes of the Church shepherded their clergy and people to vote in a Parliamentary Election of the present Italian Kingdom. . . . Last week's election statistics prove that those Italians who went to the polls are 98.28% endorsers of the 'Duce' – a record eclipsed in the U.S. only by ivory soap.

### Source I: An exiled Italian intellectual, G.A. Borgese, comments on Church–state relations.

The Church became ancillary to atheistic tyranny and tyranny rewarded it by making it supreme in the elementary cell of society, the family. Marriage and divorce became a monopoly of the Vatican, and the priest lent his hand to the squadrist in the task of perverting domestic virtues to the purpose of national violence and international anarchy. The intellectual life of the country . . . had its coup de grace from the spirit of the Inquisition and over her new black shirt Italy donned her old black gown.

### Questions

1. Explain the terms 'Catholic Action' (Source F) and 'squadrist' (Source I). [4]
2. Explain the statement 'over her new black shirt Italy donned her old black gown' (Source I). [3]
3. What do Sources F and I reveal of the benefits to the Church of the Lateran Pacts? [5]
4. How useful are Sources H and I as evidence for the historian of the results of the Lateran Pacts? [6]
*5. Using the Sources and your own knowledge, explain why the Lateran Pacts increased Mussolini's power and prestige both at home and abroad (Source G). [7]

### Worked answer

*5. [For seven marks this question requires a substantial answer, bringing in your own knowledge as well as making use of the Sources.]

Mussolini benefited from the agreement with the Church in several respects. First, as indicated in Source G, he got the credit for resolving the long-running impasse with the Church which had existed since 1870 and which no previous government had been able to end. The majority of Italians were Catholics and the agreement made them more inclined to support Mussolini, or at least to give him the benefit of the doubt.

In the lead-up to the agreements, the Papacy had already persuaded the Catholic Popolari party first to vote for the Acerbo Law and then to dissolve itself, while its more recalcitrant leaders, such as Sturzo, were exiled. This was a considerable boost to Mussolini's power. Also, as stated in Source F, bishops had to take an oath of loyalty to the state, which helped to ensure that they would be compliant.

The Pacts ensured that Mussolini would have the support of the hierarchy in the referendum of 1929; as Source H states, the clergy flocked to vote for the Fascists and exhorted their congregations to do likewise. In rural Italy especially, the clergy exerted great influence over the largely peasant population. As Source I states, 'the Church became ancillary to atheistic tyranny', condoning most of Mussolini's policies. This support was later reduced due to the disputes over Catholic Action in 1931 but Mussolini knew the Church would be reluctant to actively oppose him. Without the Lateran Pacts, this might not have been the case.

Second, the Papacy was not just an Italian but an international institution, so the agreement with the Pope gave Mussolini increased credibility abroad, for example in the favourable comments of *Time* magazine in Source H, which seems to be accepting the referendum result, though with a little scepticism about the 98 per cent figure, as a true reflection of the Duce's popularity.

Generally the agreements made the Fascist regime appear more pro-religious and respectable than was really the case. Mussolini was in reality anti-clerical but the Lateran Pacts served to disguise this fact.

# 5

# 'TRANSFORMING ITALY'

## How successful were Fascist economic and social policies?

Economics was not Mussolini's strong point and he did not have any clear views on the subject when he came to power. He devised economic policies as he went along, sometimes in response to pressure groups such as landowners and industrialists, more often for prestige, ideological or foreign policy reasons. From 1922 to 1925 he was content to allow his Minister of Finance, De Stefani, to follow the orthodox policies pursued by previous governments. De Stefani, a supporter of free trade, set out to cut the budget deficit by reducing state expenditure and restoring private ownership of utilities. Prosperity increased, thanks to the post-war economic boom and the phasing out of war debts. By the mid-1920s, industrial production had passed its wartime peak[1] and exports had doubled though this was accompanied by inflation and a balance of trade deficit.

Once Mussolini had acquired a firmer hold on power he embarked on a more radical course, signalled by De Stefani's replacement by Giuseppe Volpi, an industrialist and banker, in July 1925. From this date laissez-faire was progressively abandoned in favour of government intervention, free trade was replaced by protection and economic objectives were increasingly couched in exhortations and military terminology.

For example, in 1925 Mussolini announced the 'Battle for Grain', which, by the imposition of import duties, set out to cut the balance of payments deficit and make Italy self-sufficient in wheat. Farmers were offered large inducements to turn land over to grain production. Meanwhile, land reclamation schemes including irrigation works and new settlements were inaugurated, the best-publicized example being the drainage of the Pontine Marshes near Rome. Mussolini believed that rural life was healthier and less decadent than its urban counterpart and also that peasants were more likely to be receptive to Fascism than the industrial working class. Therefore in 1928 a ruralization policy was adopted and restrictions imposed on migration from the countryside to the towns.

Fascist initiatives were often undertaken for political and prestige reasons rather than because they made economic sense. This was the case with the revaluation of the lira. Mussolini wanted a strong currency, partly to curb inflation but primarily as a status symbol. In the 'Battle for the Lira' launched in 1927, he insisted on the so-called 'Quota 90', a new exchange rate of 90 lire to the pound, rather than the existing 150. But this artificially high exchange rate proved detrimental to the economy.

Due to government intervention, protection and a large agricultural sector, Italy suffered less than most other west European countries in the depression of 1929–32 though unemployment was still considerable. The depression was a spur to increased government spending on public works, especially the building of new highways, the *autostrade*, and of hydroelectric plants. In 1931, the Istituto Mobiliare Italiano (IMI), a business credit bank, and in 1933 the Institute for Industrial Reconstruction (IRI) were set up. The IMI had the task of bailing out private banks which were in danger of collapse in the depression, while the IRI invested directly in industry, particularly shipping, steel, shipbuilding, chemicals, electricity and telephones. By 1939 the Italian state controlled four-fifths of shipping and shipbuilding, three-quarters of iron and half of steel,[2] while as a result of the 1936 Banking Reform Act, the Bank of Italy and most other large banks became public institutions. By 1939 Italy had the highest percentage of state-owned enterprises outside the Soviet Union. Along with this went the emergence of large firms and monopolies such as Olivetti, Fiat, the Pirelli Rubber Company and Montecatini Chemicals, and of cartels between firms in the same industry to fix output and prices, practices supported by Confindustria.

From the mid-1930s, Mussolini was intent on mobilizing the economy to serve his imperial ambitions, rearmament and war. Autarky (self-sufficiency) was partly a necessity due to the League of Nations sanctions over Abyssinia, but it also resulted from Mussolini's determination to place Italy on more of a war footing. However, self-sufficiency was not achieved, nor was Italy economically equipped for war in 1940.

As discussed in chapter 4, Mussolini's most original contribution in the socio-economic sphere was the setting up of corporations, organizations of employers and workers who would collaborate in running their branch of industry. Under the Palazzo Vidoni Pact of October 1925, Confindustria and the Fascist syndicates (the only trade unions legally allowed) recognized each other as sole representatives of management and the workforce. In 1926 separate corporations for workers and employers were set up in seven branches of the economy – agriculture, banking, commerce, transport, industry, merchant marine and international commerce. Finally in 1934, twenty-two corporations, this time combining both employers and workers, were established.

Mussolini ambitiously set out to transform the ways of life and attitudes of Italians, with the aim of inculcating total obedience to the Duce and the state, together with the military and warlike characteristics essential for great-power status. Fascism had always tried to present an image of youthful virility and Mussolini considered that the best way to ensure the continuation of his regime was by indoctrinating the younger generation with Fascist ideals. Equally, he wished to train Italian youth for military service, the better to make Italy a great power. To this end a youth movement was founded in April 1926: the Opera Nazionale Balilla (ONB), called after a heroic Genoese boy who had challenged the Austrians in the Risorgimento period. Except for Catholic groups all other youth organizations were dissolved. Initially run by the Fascist Party, from 1929 the Balilla came under the control of the Ministry of Education, and teachers often doubled up as ONB officers.

Mussolini also tried to use the education system to promote Fascism. There was little direct Fascist influence on education till after 1928 when the Ministry of Public Instruction was renamed the Ministry of National Education, a more comprehensive term, since *educazione* in Italian means total upbringing. Under De Vecchi from

1935 to 1936, and Bottai from 1936 to 1943, the elementary school curriculum was revised: more physical education was introduced and textbooks were rewritten, with greater emphasis on Italian history and achievements. It was intended that 'the teacher . . . should know how to illustrate the demonstration of . . . the theories of Galileo and Marconi with remarks designed to make evident the priority and the excellence of the Italian genius'.[3] Ideology was to pervade the most unlikely subjects, as in the following arithmetic problem: '*Mussolini the teacher*. In 1902 the salary of Mussolini the teacher was 56 lire a month. How much a day? A year?'[4] Teachers had to join the Fascist Party and university teachers had to take an oath of loyalty to the regime.

Adult support for the regime was generated through an after-work organization, the Dopolavoro, established in 1925. The creation of Mario Giani, the director of Italian Westinghouse, it was originally based on the factory unit and the Fascist unions until it was taken over by the party in 1927. Membership rose from 280,000 in 1926 to four million by 1939. The Dopolavoro organized sports, outings to theatres and concerts, excursions and cheap holidays. Most towns and villages eventually possessed a Dopolavoro clubhouse with a bar, a billiard hall, a library, a radio and a cinema.

Fascism considered that women's place was in the home and their main role childbearing. As Mussolini said: 'War is to man what mother-hood is to woman'.[5] These attitudes dovetailed with the aim of increasing the birth rate; in 1927 Mussolini had proclaimed the 'Battle for Births', stating: 'Italy, if she is to count for anything in the world, must have a population of not less than 60 million inhabitants [from 40 million] by the middle of this century.'[6] A tax on bachelors was imposed and marriage loans, redeemable after a certain number of children had been born, marriage grants, and family allowances for two or more children, were introduced. There was a special Day of the Mother and Child and ceremonial awards for large families. Contraception, sterilization and abortion were all banned.

Meanwhile, efforts were made to exclude women from education and work, especially from professional jobs and state employment. In 1938 a 10 per cent female quota was imposed in public administration and large and medium-sized firms, though the war soon made this unenforceable.

With these views, there was little room for women in the Fascist Party. The Fasci Femminili founded in the 1920s attracted some middle-class women who engaged in voluntary and charitable activities, but apart from some mother and child groups, most women remained outside the party structure and the few within it were allowed no part in policy-making.

## ANALYSIS (1): HOW EFFECTIVE WERE MUSSOLINI'S POLICIES IN RESOLVING ITALY'S ECONOMIC AND SOCIAL PROBLEMS?

Mussolini did not significantly improve either the Italian economy or overall standards of living. He sometimes claimed that this had never been his intention, arguing that he aimed to create a hardy, self-sacrificing race, rather than a prosperous one. He stated in 1936: 'we must rid our minds of the idea that what we have called the days of prosperity may return. We are probably moving towards a period when humanity will exist on a lower standard of living.'[7] Fascist economic policy was indeed motivated more by prestige than by economic or social needs. But even judged on its declared objectives of preparing Italy for empire and territorial expansion, it was not a success.

The regime's agricultural policies did little to modernize farming methods or to increase productivity. The 'Battle for Grain' proved counter-productive since much marginal land, some of it with unsuitable climate and soil, was turned over to wheat production. As a result output increased from 5.39 million tonnes in 1925 to 7.27 million in 1935,[8] and Italy covered 75 per cent of its grain requirements by 1939, but this was at the expense of higher food prices and declining export crops. Olives, fruit and vines, which could have provided the foreign credits to buy imported wheat at lower prices, were abandoned in many areas in favour of grain. Productivity fell, and the only real beneficiaries were large farmers who gained from increased rents and prices.

Land reclamation programmes had promised 'land to the peasants', but this did not materialize. The Pontine Marshes scheme was the exception rather than the rule. Overall, only 10,000 people were settled on reclaimed land. One difficulty was that the projects tended to be run by consortia with insufficient capital and most were not even begun till 1939. The main benefit of the reclamation schemes was in providing employment in public works during the depression.

Mussolini's ruralization policy was quite incompatible with his aim of expanding Italy's industrial base. There was a further contradiction in that higher wheat production was best achieved on large estates rather than the small peasant holdings idealized by the Fascists. The outcome was that land holdings became concentrated in fewer hands and the numbers of peasant smallholders actually decreased relative to tenants and sharecroppers. In spite of the ban on moving to towns, peasants continued to vote with their feet and the rural population declined while that of industrial centres grew – for example, the population of Milan increased by more than 40 per cent between 1921 and 1934.[9]

One of the most intractable difficulties faced by Italian governments was the north–south divide and the extreme poverty of Italy's southern provinces. But Mussolini paid scant attention to the southern problem, and the gap between north and south actually widened under his regime. US immigration restrictions, introduced in the 1920s, had cut off the south's traditional safety valve of emigration, while the expansion of industry in the north (half of all industrial workers were in north-west Italy) made the contrast with the southern provinces more pronounced. There was no land reform to alleviate the lot of landless labourers and little investment. Landowners in northern Italy gained most from Fascist agricultural policy.

The fortunes of industry under Fascism were more mixed. In 1927 the revaluation of the lira at clearly too high a level had deleterious results for export industries, leading to deflationary policies and wage cuts. However, Italy suffered rather less from the depression than most industrialized countries; the IMI and IRI were successful in preventing a banking collapse and providing credit for industry, while public works kept the unemployment figures down. Nevertheless, there were still between one and two million Italians unemployed in the early 1930s amounting to about 15 per cent of the working population (compared with 22 per cent in the UK and 30 per cent in Germany). Government figures understated the total, since they excluded some groups such as agricultural workers and it is likely that unemployment did not drop below 700,000 till 1939.[10]

Mussolini claimed that under his regime Italy was developing into a modern industrial society, backed by extensive state intervention. A newspaper article by his brother Arnaldo in September 1926 stated:

> The Italian bourgeoisie has . . . failed to perform its task. . . . This is the century of chemicals and electricity. We can't sit for ever in the epoch of iron and steam. . . . Private enterprise has not shown resilience in its plans, methods and initiatives. The Fascist state has intervened in its place.[11]

Industry certainly expanded (though this would most likely have happened irrespective of Fascism), but what was distinctive about Mussolini's economic policy was the high level of state-financed investment in heavy industry. The IMI and especially the IRI were among the regime's most innovative and successful ventures and from 1936 increasing amounts of investment capital came from state-owned financial institutions rather than private sources. The aim was to develop capital goods and war production industries, protected by tariffs from external competition. These policies met with some success. By 1938 industrial production was back at 1929 levels, though accompanied by a large budget deficit and depleted currency reserves. Shipbuilding, chemicals and engineering all thrived. Output of iron and steel trebled from 1918 to 1940, hydroelectric power increased and 5,000 kilometres of railway were electrified, a basis for the boast that under Fascism the trains ran on time. However, this was at the expense of export and consumer goods industries whose interests were disregarded, with a resultant decline in textiles and problems for the car industry in selling abroad – Fiat exported fewer cars in the late 1930s than in the 1920s.[12]

Despite Mussolini's efforts, economic growth under Fascism was not very impressive. From a base line of 100 in 1922, the growth index reached 204 by 1929 but a decade later stood at only 208. Nor was there any evidence of increased productivity. Economic gains had been promised from the conquest of Abyssinia, but few materialized from this or other foreign adventures. Mussolini over-optimistically aimed to make Italy self-sufficient in raw materials to overcome shortages of coal, oil and natural gas. As he said:

> I consider the Italian nation in a permanent state of war . . . to live for me means struggle, risk, stubbornness . . . never to submit to destiny, not even to . . . our so-called deficiency in raw materials. Even this deficiency can be overcome by other raw materials.[13]

From 1936, bilateral trade agreements, foreign currency controls, raw materials allocation controls and an import licensing system with quotas were introduced. Though some progress was made in the manufacture of synthetic fibres, as well as in energy supply with the discovery by the state-owned oil corporation of natural gas in the Po valley, self-sufficiency in essential raw materials was never attained. The main result of these policies was greater reliance on trade with Germany; imports from Italy's new ally increased from 18 per cent in 1936 to 29 per cent in 1940, and by the late 1930s, 25 per cent of Italian exports went to Germany and a further 25 per cent to Africa. But ominously, in 1940 Italy still lagged well behind Germany, France and Belgium in production of capital goods and war materials. It produced only 1 million tonnes each of iron and steel compared with 13.9 million tonnes of iron and 19 million tonnes of steel in Germany, and 1.8 million tonnes of iron and 1.9 million tonnes of steel in Belgium.[14] Italy's share of world manufacturing output had actually declined from 3.3 per cent in 1929 to 2.9 per cent in 1938, while Germany, Japan and the USSR had all improved their relative positions over the same period.[15] Despite all Mussolini's efforts, Italy was economically ill equipped for war.

Nor did state investment mean that the government acquired real power over the economy. It has been said that Fascist Italy had 'control over the labour movement and very little control over the nation's economic structure'.[16] Private ownership continued and employers largely retained their independence; Mussolini did not dare offend the owners of land or large businesses on whose support he depended.

Poverty and low standards of living were major social problems when Mussolini came to power, but he did little to address these issues and in practice workers lost rights rather than acquiring them. At first, some of the more radical Fascist union leaders such as Edmondo Rossoni took industrial action over wage demands and working conditions, an example of this being the Valdarno miners' strike in August 1924. But the Fascist unions were not backed by the government or the party and were disadvantaged by the fact that their leaders were not elected but appointed from above. Strikes were prohibited in 1926 and the interests of the employers invariably prevailed.

There is little evidence that, overall, the standards of living of workers and peasants improved under Fascism. Any benefits from representation in the corporations were more than offset by wage cuts of 10 per cent in 1927 (the result of the revaluation of the lira) and 12 per cent in the depression of 1930. This was a period of falling prices, and wages increased when prices rose again in the later 1930s. But only in 1938 did they regain their pre-Fascist levels and it is estimated that from 1925 to 1938 real wages probably declined by 11 per cent, while agricultural workers' wages may have fallen by 20–40 per cent in the early 1930s.

Against this has to be set the introduction of a shorter (forty-hour) working week, paid holidays, sick pay and increases in piecework rates for workers in selected industries. A Labour Charter was introduced in April 1927 which paid lip service to employment rights, settlement of disputes, rights on dismissal, Sundays off, paid holidays, sick pay and insurance, though most of these provisions were not implemented. Some social reforms were introduced such as sickness insurance in 1928 and disability benefits, while the expansion of elementary education helped reduce the illiteracy rate, though it remained high in the south. The emphasis on the birth rate and antenatal care led to more spending on health.

Workers in heavy industry undoubtedly gained more than those in consumer goods industries and much more than those in agriculture.

But the main beneficiaries of Fascist social policy were the middle and lower middle class, who filled the increasing number of white-collar jobs in the public sector and in the Fascist Party bureaucracy; the number of public employees doubled in the 1930s from 500,000 to one million.[17] The main outcome of occupational change was to increase the income gap between the middle and working classes and the gulf between town and country.

During the war there was much greater hardship for all groups but especially for the urban working class. Rationing was introduced in May 1939 and extended to pasta and bread in 1940 and 1941, and the resulting food shortages, black market and later the bombing raids on Italian cities caused great discontent, culminating in extensive strikes in Turin and Milan in March 1943.

Therefore, while the Fascist period saw more industrialization and an increase in state financing of selected industries, it did not succeed in improving Italy's relative economic status. Expansion of some sectors of industry was at the expense of decline elsewhere, and little was done to resolve agricultural problems or to increase overall prosperity.

## Questions

1. 'Its achievements, outside the field of propaganda, were a sham.' Discuss this verdict on Mussolini's economic and social policy between 1926 and 1940.
2. Which groups in the Italian population gained most from Mussolini's economic and social policies?

## ANALYSIS (2): TO WHAT EXTENT DID THE FASCIST REGIME SUCCEED IN BRINGING ABOUT A 'SOCIAL REVOLUTION' IN ITALY?

Mussolini's 'revolution' turned out to be one of style rather than substance.[18] He had aimed to inculcate the population with Fascist beliefs while at the same time 'remaking' Italians into a hardy, disciplined and united race. But these objectives were, at best, only partially achieved. There was in any case a relatively short period of time in which to implement changes, since most initiatives did not get underway till the mid- or late 1920s, but even so there is little evidence that, under Fascism, Italian life or attitudes were fundamentally altered.

The most pervasive agencies of Fascist social change were the Balilla and Dopolavoro but these were not as all-embracing or influential as their membership figures indicate. The Balilla encompassed age groups from 6 upwards, starting with the Order of the Wolf for 6–8-year-olds, through the Balilla proper for ages 8 to 13, to the Avanguardisti for 14–18-year-olds, and thence to the Young Fascists (the Fasci Giovanili). There were parallel organizations for girls, though these were less important. In 1937 the Balilla, the Fasci Giovanili and university students were all brought together in one organization, the Gioventù Italiana del Littorio. By 1937 it was compulsory to belong to the Balilla and at its peak it claimed a membership of eight million. It organized sports and physical education, after-school activities, excursions and summer camps, and its uniformed members met every Saturday afternoon for parades and military drill.

The Balilla claimed a participation rate of between 60 and 70 per cent of 6–18-year-olds but not all members attended meetings regularly and the figures concealed considerable regional, age and gender variations. The Fascist youth movement seems to have been most popular with middle-class boys living in urban areas. Membership was lowest in south/central Italy, especially in rural areas where the influence of the state was weakest. Fewer girls belonged, probably because female activities were more circumscribed and therefore less attractive. The great majority of working-class and peasant children had in any case left school by the age of 11 and membership also declined after the age of 18, from 74 per cent to 53 per cent of males in 1936.[19]

It is also doubtful how far the Balilla succeeded in its objective of converting Italian youth to Fascist beliefs. While there was considerable emphasis on promoting the cult of the Duce and on military training, the main attraction for its members seems to have been its non-political leisure pursuits, outings and sport. One of the Balilla's aims was to break down class barriers but this rarely occurred in practice since its activities were based on schools, which usually had separate social catchment areas.

Also, Catholic Action groups continued to provide an alternative source of leisure activities, with up to 388,000 estimated members by 1939.[20] The compromise of 1931 had allowed these youth groups to survive, though in somewhat truncated form, providing they did not organize athletics or sports. They were strongest in private and Catholic schools.

Changes to the education system were slow to get off the ground. Early educational reforms introduced by Gentile in 1923 had followed a traditional model, emphasizing humanities over science and reducing the numbers going to secondary school or university. In education the impact of the curriculum changes was mitigated by the early school-leaving age as well as by still widespread illiteracy – as late as 1939, 40 per cent of the population in Sicily, Calabria and Basilicata were estimated to be unable to read or write.[21] Also the educational innovations mostly affected elementary schools and did not permeate secondary and higher education to the same extent.

Four million Italians, comprising about 40 per cent of the workforce, were estimated to be in the Dopolavoro by 1939.[22] This institution was undoubtedly popular, though more with the lower middle class than the working class, and with men rather than with women, since most women did not work and those who did had less time or inclination to attend after-work events. Figures for 1936 estimate that 20 per cent of urban workers, 7 per cent of rural workers and 80 per cent of state employees belonged.[23] Its main attraction was its recreational and entertainment programmes, and overt propaganda tended to be played down. Like the Balilla, there were usually separate class activities. Historians consider that the Dopolavoro served to distract attention from social problems and may have helped promote consensus among the working population but was a lot less successful in embedding Fascist values.

Fascism prescribed a subservient role for women but this attitude was not new and not specific to the ideology. Italy had never had a strong feminist movement and the Catholic Church had always held very traditional views on women's position. It is likely that the attitudes of Italian women were as much, if not more, influenced by the Church than by Fascism. Likewise, attempts to reduce female employment in the depression were a feature of most western economies and not unique to Italy.

Despite the attempts to remove women from the workforce, there was no great decline in female employment over the Fascist period; the proportion of women working fell from 33 per cent in 1922 to 28 per cent in 1936 (as much a result of the depression as of Fascist policies), and rose slightly thereafter.[24] In 1922 about half of Italian women workers were employed in agriculture and many of the remainder in the textile industries. By 1939, this pattern had changed and more women were now employed in white-collar jobs in the service industries or in teaching. The government tried to prevent women from working in office jobs where they competed with men, but there were fewer restrictions on working-class jobs. Legislation, such as the 1938 law putting a quota of 10 per cent on women in public employment and the professions, was difficult to enforce. In any case it quickly became a dead letter during the war, which necessitated the substitution of women for men in numerous occupations, including public service. Equally, urbanization and American cultural influences in magazines and films may have acted as a counterweight to state ideology.[25] Despite disapproval of women in higher education, the female university population actually increased from 6 per cent in 1914 to 20 per cent in 1938.

Fascism also signally failed in its aim of increasing the birth rate. Despite some financial inducements, the population only rose from 38,450,000 in 1921 to 44,900,000 in 1950, much less than the 60 million target of the 'Battle for Births', and part of the increase resulted from the decline in emigration.

Nor did Fascism make much of an impact on cultural life, the exception being architecture where a mixture of 'rational' and 'Mussolini modern' styles with classical and imperial designs was introduced, and plans were made for the rebuilding of much of Rome. Some attempts to impose Fascist cultural changes met with open hostility. For example, the attempted introduction of the Fascist salute in 1937 and the substitution of *voi* for the formal *lei* as a form of address in 1938 were derided and generally ignored. A major constraint on social change was the existence of Catholicism as an alternative value system. There is little doubt that many Italians looked for guidance to the Church rather than to the Duce.

Fascism's attempts to transform Italy therefore fell well short of a 'social revolution'. There was more success in north and central Italy, in urban areas and among the middle class (who were getting most out of the regime). The rural south with its peasant population was much less influenced by Fascist institutions. Historians conclude that attempts to bring about social change were necessarily limited, 'the Fascist government had neither the means nor the self-confidence to force through unpopular policies',[26] and many areas of life remained largely untouched by Fascism.

## Questions

1. 'A reformer but an incompetent one.' Discuss this opinion of Mussolini in the light of his aims and achievements from 1925 to 1940.
2. Was radical reform a significant feature of Mussolini's domestic policy?

# SOURCES

## 1. WORKING AND LIVING CONDITIONS IN FASCIST ITALY

### Source A: The Labour Charter, April 1927.

Art. 7 The Corporate State regards private initiative in the field of production as the most useful and efficient instrument for furthering the interests of the nation. . . .

From the fact that the elements of production (labour and capital) are co-operators in a common enterprise, reciprocal rights and duties devolve upon them.

Art. 9 State intervention in economic production arises only when private enterprise is lacking or insufficient, or when the political interests of the state are involved . . .

Art. 15 The employee has the right to a weekly day of rest, falling on Sundays. . . .

Art. 16 After a year of uninterrupted service, the employee in enterprises that function the year round is entitled to an annual vacation with pay. . . .

### Source B: The Labour and Anti-strike Law, 1926.

Art. 18 The lockout and the strike are prohibited.

### Source C: A Fascist union leader, Edmondo Rossoni, gives his views on industrial relations in December 1922.

Between Italians and Italians there should be neither masters nor servants, but loyal collaborators for the common interest and for the over-riding ends of the Fatherland . . . against the 'bosses' in the old sense of the word we shall fight ruthlessly.

### Source D: A Fascist party official comments on the results of Fascist policy in 1943.

The Charter of Labour. What the objects of your social legislation were supposed to be I shall not even mention. One can decide whether or not they have been achieved by a dispassionate examination of their results: . . .

The duplication of bodies with the function of regulating individual sectors of the economy (how many offices are now responsible for cereals, beverages, etc.?)

An increase in the number of plutocrats and in the power of plutocracies. . . .

Chaos in the provision and distribution of raw materials and basic foods.

### Source E: Togliatti (the exiled Italian Communist leader) comments on the role of the Dopolavoro. Quoted from Togliatti's lectures in Moscow in 1935.

What do the local *Dopolavoros* do? They carry on a whole series of activities. The benefits the workers have are manifold. They get special terms, reductions for theatre and movie tickets, discounts on food and clothing bought in certain department stores, on outings. Then they also get some form of welfare. In some cases, the *Dopolavoro* tends to take on mutual-aid functions and assists, for example, needy families of disabled workers, etc., etc.

It's time to stop thinking the workers shouldn't engage in sports. Even the smallest advantages are not scorned by the workers. . . . Just being able to sit in a room and listen to the radio in the evening is something that brings pleasure. We cannot inveigh against the worker who agrees to enter this room for the mere fact that the Fascist symbol is on the door.

## Questions

1.  Define the Corporate State (Source A) and the Dopolavoro (Source E) [4]
2.  What do Sources A and E reveal of the benefits to Italian workers of Fascist labour policy and legislation? [4]
*3. To what extent are Rossoni's claims in Source C refuted by the evidence of Sources A, B and D? [5]
4.  How valuable as evidence for the historian of the success of Mussolini's social policies are Sources D and E? [5]
5.  Using all the Sources and your own knowledge, assess to what extent working and living conditions improved under Fascism. [7]

## Worked answer

*3. [You should look at what Rossoni says and then at the other three Sources in turn, focusing on the extent to which they support or refute Rossoni's view.]

Rossoni in Source C is optimistic that employers and workers will be able to work together on equal terms in Fascist Italy. Also he is confident that workers in the Fascist unions will be able to hold their own against the more reactionary 'bosses'.

However, Source A only partly supports this view. The Labour Charter does envisage workers and employers as equals, both playing a role in the running of the enterprise and both having rights and duties. Furthermore, workers appear to be legally guaranteed improvements in working conditions such as a day off on Sunday and paid holidays. However, other clauses in Source A indicate that employers will still be the decision-makers and will still dominate the corporations. For example, art. 7 states that private enterprise is the desirable form of industrial organization and art. 9 says that the state will only intervene in the running of industry as a last resort.

Source B goes further, banning strikes (though, to add balance, it also prohibits lockouts), so that Rossoni's unions would in practice be ineffective in bringing pressure to bear on employers.

Rossoni is writing at the start of the Fascist period, but the actual outcome of economic policies can be seen in Source D. True, this is written during the war, when Italians faced numerous hardships and shortages, but it contradicts Rossoni's optimistic assumptions, stating that the Labour Charter has brought benefits not to workers but only to the wealthy and powerful (the plutocrats). It has also led to increased bureaucracy and a proliferation of competing and overlapping agencies. The evidence of these Sources is that Rossoni's dream of equal partnership was far from being realized.

# SOURCES

## 2. ITALIAN YOUTH UNDER FASCISM

### Source F: The aims of the Balilla.

It diffuses throughout all social strata that training in arms which has restored to honour the virtue of courage, personal responsibility and initiative. Its action is far reaching, incessant and progressive. Instruction, gymnastics, sport, camping, cruises, military exercises, artistic and musical activities and excursions all tend to create an atmosphere of equality, emulation and solidarity, which has not been achieved by any other institution in the world.

### Source G: The rules of the Balilla.

Oath: In the name of God and Italy I swear to carry out the orders of the DUCE and to serve with all my strength and, if necessary, with my blood, the Cause of the Fascist Revolution.

Rule 12: When one finds oneself in the presence of people, even adults, who cast doubt on the fundamental political principles of the Regime, or who express lack of faith in its Leaders, and when there is no other older person there, one . . . must intervene to correct, and if necessary, scold and silence anyone who holds an offensive attitude to the Regime.

### Source H: The role of youth under Fascism (an extract from a Fascist youth bulletin in 1931).

it was necessary to found the Fasci Giovanili as direct heirs of the Action Squads, as a great training ground for the spirits and muscles to rear the future soldiers of the Fatherland. . . . It is among the young that all great movements in history have found their prophets, their soldiers, their martyrs . . . it is the unquestioning support of the young which vouches for the value and universality of a movement. . . . Seeing the Young Fascists in the squares of Italy and hearing their songs, we who are concerned for the fate of the Regime have our conviction reaffirmed . . . that Fascism is universal and that no force will ever stop its progress.

**Source I: Membership of the Balilla in June 1939.**

Boys and girls 6–7        1,355,575
Boys 8–13               1,576,925
Girls 8–13              1,501,834
Boys 14–17                756,236
Girls 14–17               387,321
Boys 18–21                745,608
Girls 18–21               378,140

National average membership 50% of age group.
South membership 36% of age group.

**Source J: Reports written in 1931 and 1937 by the provincial party secretary in Turin, to Starace, the national party secretary.**

unfortunately, instead of diminishing, the detachment between Fascism and the youth sector seems to be growing. . . . [There] is an aversion to what Fascism represents and a repulsion for the idea of coming closer and understanding what Fascism really means. . . . The young Fascists are deserting the meetings. . . . Only the books are full of members, but the truth is that the young no longer go to the groups.

**Questions**

1.  Identify the Duce (Source G). [2]
2.  What information is contained in Sources F, G and H about the aims of the Fascist youth movement? [6]
3.  Referring to Sources F and G, explain what attractions the Balilla may have had for Italian youth. [4]
*4. How useful are Sources I and J as evidence for the historian regarding the success of the Balilla? [5]
5.  Using all the Sources and your own knowledge, assess the success of Fascist youth policies. [8]

**Worked answer**

*4. *[In evaluating Source J as evidence for the historian it is useful to look at the date/s, the author and the purpose of his report. Also, remember that statistics, while factual, have their own limitations as evidence.]*

Source I, the list of membership figures, is a factual piece of evidence and provides information on the participation rates of different age groups and of males and females. It is also informative on the lower Balilla participation in southern Italy. These figures are corroborated by other sources. However, these statistical data do not reveal how many members were active and actually attended meetings or how regularly, or how committed to Fascism they were. It is therefore an incomplete description of the impact and effectiveness of the Balilla. The historian would have to resort to qualitative sources of evidence to obtain a fuller picture of the success of the Balilla.

Source I is not supported by Source J which takes the view that the Balilla was not achieving its aims, even in terms of membership. This source is highly pessimistic about the success of the Balilla, an unusual perspective for a Fascist Party official, who we would expect to be more positive in his reports to the party secretary (perhaps he had an ulterior motive in presenting the most gloomy scenario). However, he would be in a good position to know what was happening in his region and his opinion that most Italian youths were repelled by Fascist indoctrination is backed up by other evidence from the period, though as Turin was a main northern industrial centre one would expect Balilla participation to be greater here than in most parts of Italy. A further limitation is that this source refers only to Turin and therefore cannot necessarily be extrapolated to provide a picture of the success of the Balilla over the whole country.

# 6

# 'GREAT, RESPECTED AND FEARED'

## How successful was Mussolini's foreign policy from 1922 to 1938?

### BACKGROUND NARRATIVE

Mussolini had been propounding nationalist views for several years before 1922, so it is not surprising that his ambition when he came to power was, as he said, to make Italy 'great, respected and feared', though this was more a general aim than a detailed set of policies. In Fascist Italy, it was certainly Mussolini who made the major foreign policy decisions. He was his own Foreign Minister for much of the Fascist era, and his son-in-law, Galeazzo Ciano, when appointed to the post in 1936, was obliged to defer to Mussolini on most important issues. To begin with, the Duce was content to be guided by the foreign office staff, but he soon decided to ignore them, just as he usually disregarded the advice of his generals and commanders-in-chief. In 1933 he took over the War, Navy and Airforce ministries, gaining greater powers over the armed forces, though to Mussolini's annoyance they still owed their first loyalty to the King.

One of the questions to consider about foreign policy in the Fascist era is how far it resulted from Mussolini's personal preferences and personality, and how far from traditional Italian objectives. Mussolini liked to think that his foreign policy was entirely original, but in fact there was considerable continuity with that of previous liberal governments. Like them, Mussolini sought to further Italian interests in the Adriatic, the Mediterranean and North and East Africa (see Map 2). However, while his objectives were similar, Mussolini's style and methods were quite different from those of his predecessors. Ignoring Italy's economic and military weaknesses, he was impulsive, inconsistent and erratic. He valued prestige more than anything else and was never satisfied unless he was in the limelight playing a leading role. He was to become increasingly fond of making grandiloquent statements such as 'better to live one day as a lion than a thousand years as a lamb',[1] and declaring that war was not only inevitable but also desirable, adding 'the character of the Italian people must be moulded by fighting'.[2] With a 'tendency to view European diplomacy through the eyes of a newspaper editor',[3] he aimed at spectacular gestures without much thought for consequences, resulting in a foreign policy that has been described as 'by turn ambivalent, futile and malignant'.[4]

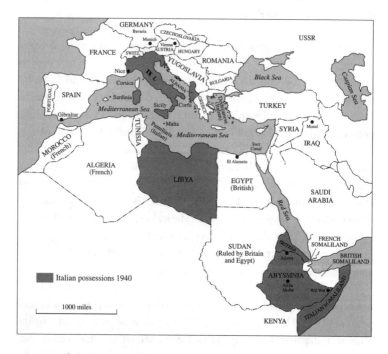

*Map 2* Italy in international and colonial affairs.
*Source:* A. Cassels: *Fascist Italy* (London: Routledge & Kegan Paul, 1969)

These characteristics were less apparent in the 1920s than they were later. When Mussolini first came to power he had to work within the constraints imposed by Britain and France, the victors in the First World War and the strongest European powers in the 1920s. Britain dominated the Mediterranean, controlling Gibraltar, Malta and Suez, while France possessed extensive North African colonies. The western powers in turn needed Italian cooperation in creating post-war stability, just as they later hoped for Italian support to restrain Hitler's Germany. Mussolini in the 1920s was largely content to collaborate with the western democracies, for example in the Locarno Agreements of October 1925. He used diplomacy to make some modest gains such as the acquisition of Fiume and minor territorial changes in East Africa. In June 1933 he tried to engineer a pact with Britain, France and Germany whereby these four powers would determine European affairs in cooperation but it never came into effect.

But even in this period Mussolini's diplomacy was interspersed with acts of aggression such as the occupation of Corfu in August 1923 in retaliation for the murder of some Italians on the Greek–Albanian border. He also tried to undermine the new state of Yugoslavia, and sided with other revisionist powers such as Hungary and Austria which had suffered territorial losses as a result of the war.

Mussolini also encouraged German right-wing parties but, after Hitler came to power in 1933, relations were strained despite ideological similarities. The Duce's first meeting with the new German leader in Venice in June 1934 was not a success. Mussolini resented Nazi assumptions of racial superiority and feared lest Nazism might come to rival Fascism. While he sought a German revival to counter-balance Britain and France, this was more than outweighed by his fear of Anschluss, German–Austrian union, which would create a Greater Germany on the Italian frontier and thus counteract Italy's gains at Versailles. To safeguard against this, he was anxious to have Austria as a client state and backed Chancellor Dollfuss in establishing an anti-German government along Fascist lines. In February 1934 Dollfuss set up a one-party state and suppressed the Socialist opposition but in July he was assassinated by Austrian Nazis. Mussolini immediately moved troops to the frontier in a show of anti-German strength and Hitler was forced to abandon this first attempt to absorb Austria into the Reich. When in March 1935 Hitler contravened the Versailles

Treaty by announcing German rearmament and possession of an airforce, Italy joined Britain and France in the Stresa Front. This agreement of April 1935 committed the three powers to resist any treaty violations and to support Austrian independence.

The Stresa Front had already been weakened by the Anglo-German Naval Agreement of June 1935 which allowed Germany to build a navy well in excess of that permitted at Versailles, but it fell apart completely when Mussolini launched an invasion of Abyssinia in October 1935. Contrary to his expectations, the League of Nations imposed economic sanctions which, while inadequate to prevent the conquest of Abyssinia, estranged Mussolini from the western powers, and resulted in a closer relationship between Italy and Germany.

Abyssinia was a watershed in Mussolini's foreign policy. From this time on he became increasingly pro-German, and the friendship was cemented by joint aid to the Nationalists in the Spanish Civil War. When General Franco led a rebellion against the left-wing Spanish republic in July 1936, he applied to Italy for help and Mussolini immediately decided to send planes to transport the Nationalists' Moroccan army to mainland Spain. He followed this up with further substantial aid throughout the three-year war, eventually sending 60,000 troops along with tanks and munitions. Italian intervention was undertaken mainly to forestall a Communist take-over in Spain and to weaken France (whose Popular Front government was ideologically similar to that of the Spanish republic) but Mussolini also had more grandiose ambitions. He dreamed of re-establishing a Mediterranean Roman Empire, creating a satellite state in Spain and acquiring naval bases in the Balearic Islands. However, he was to be disappointed for Italy gained little from the war. Italian troops performed badly at first and intervention cost 12–14 million lire, and one-third of Italy's available arms. Franco's regime was superficially modelled on Fascism but the Spanish leader kept power firmly in his own hands and was adept at avoiding repaying his obligations to his allies. Meanwhile disputes over non-intervention (a British–French initiative to which Italy had also nominally agreed), and Italian submarine attacks on merchant shipping bound for Spain further strained relations with the western powers and ensured that Mussolini would move further into the German sphere.

From 1936, Mussolini gradually abandoned his earlier policy and gave Hitler what was virtually a free hand to implement the Anschluss.

In January 1936, he conceded that Austria would be a German satellite. In October Ciano signed the Rome–Berlin Protocols, an agreement which became known as the Axis – a focal point around which all other European states would revolve. A secret understanding demarcated Italy's sphere of influence as the Mediterranean and Germany's as eastern Europe. In September 1937 Mussolini made what he regarded as a triumphal state visit to Germany; in November 1937 he joined the Anti-Comintern Pact, an anti-Soviet agreement signed the previous year between Germany and Japan, and in December Italy left the League of Nations.

The Anschluss finally occurred in March 1938. As a result of German pressure on Austria, Chancellor Schuschnigg called a referendum to reaffirm Austrian independence. But before it could be held German troops mobilized on the frontier, Schuschnigg resigned and a Nazi, Seyss-Inquart, became Chancellor in his place. German troops marched in on 12 March and Austria was annexed to the Reich. Mussolini had not been consulted but he made the best of a bad job, despite the fact that the Anschluss allowed German expansion south-eastwards to the Italian frontier, the outcome he had made great efforts to prevent only four years earlier.

The acquisition of Austria put Hitler in a better strategic position to undermine his next victim, Czechoslovakia, and he began laying claim to the largely German-speaking Sudetenland. War appeared to be imminent after two failed meetings with the British Prime Minister, Neville Chamberlain, at Berchtesgaden and Godesberg in September 1938, but it was averted at the last moment at the Munich Conference on 29 September. Here Mussolini had a rare opportunity to pose as a peace-maker, mediating between Hitler and the western powers, though in fact he merely underwrote the German aims when Hitler was allocated the Sudetenland without having to go to war for it.

The way had been paved for a German–Italian alliance. But far from being in control of events as he had anticipated, Mussolini was now subordinate to Hitler, a role which was to drag him into an ultimately disastrous war.

## ANALYSIS (1): HOW FAR WAS THE PERIOD 1922 TO 1932 'A DECADE OF GOOD BEHAVIOUR' IN ITALIAN FOREIGN POLICY?

Mussolini followed a fairly moderate and restrained foreign policy in this period, but more out of necessity than conviction. He had to work within the limitations of Italian diplomatic and military weakness at a time when Britain and France dominated European affairs. Also, up to 1926 he was more preoccupied with consolidating his position within Italy than with foreign policy. The pacification of Libya tied up a good part of the army in the 1920s, while the 1929 depression necessitated cuts in military spending.

Though Italy had ambitions in the Mediterranean (*mare nostrum*, as it was described), Africa and the Balkans, during these 'quiet years' Mussolini generally found it expedient to cooperate with the western powers in resolving post-war problems. Italy joined Britain and France in underwriting the Locarno Agreements of 1925 which guaranteed Germany's post-Versailles frontiers with France and Belgium, though, surprisingly, it did not mention the Italian–Austrian frontier. Along with most other European powers, Mussolini recognized the Soviet Union in the mid-1920s. Italy was a dutiful member of the League of Nations and in 1928 endorsed the Kellogg–Briand Pact, a Franco-American initiative which committed its signatories to renounce war, though few states, including Italy, took it seriously – Mussolini said the Pact was 'so sublime that it should be called transcendental'.[5] Italy also made constructive contributions to the 1930–2 Geneva Disarmament Conference. These developments seemed to show that Mussolini was a responsible statesman seeking to preserve peace. It even seemed that some revision of Versailles might be achieved amicably when Italy at last acquired Fiume as a result of an agreement with Yugoslavia in January 1924; or when, also in 1924, it negotiated for small pieces of French and British territory to be added to the Italian colonies of Libya and Somaliland.

But there were also indications in this period that Mussolini was looking for trouble. The first and most dramatic example of this was the Italian occupation of the Greek island of Corfu in August 1923. This arose out of the murder on Greek territory of five Italians who were working for the Greek–Albanian boundary commission. Mussolini blamed the Greeks and sent an ultimatum demanding an apology, the bringing to justice of the perpetrators and compensation of 50 million lire. When the Greek government refused to accept all these conditions he sent the Italian fleet to bombard and occupy Corfu. In fact the boundary commission incident was largely a pretext. Corfu occupied a strategic position in the Adriatic and Mussolini was already planning to take it over as a bargaining counter in his dispute with Greece over the Dodecanese Islands – Greek-populated islands which had been acquired by Italy in 1912.

Greece appealed to the League of Nations but, faced with this first serious challenge to its authority, the League chose to refer the problem to the lower-profile Conference of Ambassadors (a body established at Versailles to deal with disputes arising from the peace conference). Eventually, a compromise was reached whereby Greece paid compensation and Mussolini reluctantly evacuated Corfu. Though he had had to relinquish his conquest, Mussolini claimed a diplomatic victory and the incident revealed his contempt for international opinion and his willingness to resort to force in order to achieve his ends.

In furtherance of his Adriatic ambitions Mussolini also intervened in Albania, a recently created and weak Balkan state. He engineered the rise to power of his protégé King Zog in 1926 and the ensuing friendship treaty led to Albania becoming an Italian client state, granting Italy oil and other economic concessions in return for military aid. By acquiring this foothold on the Adriatic coast, Mussolini hoped to weaken Yugoslavia, the beneficiary of much of the Austro-Hungarian territory Italy had demanded at Versailles. He aided Croat separatists with arms and money after 1929 and bore some responsibility for the assassination by Italian-financed Croats of the Yugoslav King and the French Foreign Minister in Marseilles in 1934.

Mussolini's co-operation with the western powers could not disguise his underlying hostility to France, from which Italy had long-standing claims to Nice, Corsica and Sardinia. Mussolini, jealous of the French North African empire, clashed over the rights of Italians living in the French colonies and encouraged opposition movements in Tunisia and Morocco. By an anti-Yugoslav policy he hoped to weaken the French Little Entente, the agreements France had made with Yugoslavia and other successor states created at Versailles. Mussolini also pursued a policy of friendship with states which had been on the losing side in the First World War, for example Hungary, with which he concluded a treaty in 1927, Austria and Germany. He thus followed a dual policy of contributing to European stability on the one hand, while seeking covertly to undermine it on the other. Despite this, Mussolini's latest biographer avers that 'to 1932, Italian diplomacy under his dictatorship remained more Italian than anything else; in so far as foreign affairs were concerned, Mussolini administered a system rather than crafting a new policy of his own free will'.[6]

Mussolini's tactics in this period brought a few tangible gains, but there were no really worthwhile concessions of the kind he coveted, for example African colonies or the Middle East mandates which Italy had been denied at Versailles. Hence he became increasingly reckless in pursuit of his foreign and imperial ambitions. He began talking about 'Fascism for export',[7] and claimed that 'a nation to remain healthy should make war every twenty-five years'.[8] Though not implemented till 1935, the conquest of Abyssinia was planned much earlier. And when Mussolini took over from Grandi as Foreign Minister in 1932 the way was paved for a much more overtly aggressive policy.

### Question

1.  How far is it correct to say that even in his first decade Mussolini was 'a disrupter of the stability of Europe'?

### ANALYSIS (2): 'A PLACE IN THE SUN': WHY, AND WITH WHAT CONSEQUENCES, DID MUSSOLINI DECIDE TO INVADE ABYSSINIA?

In a speech in March 1934, Mussolini had announced that 'the historical objectives of Italy have two names: Asia and Africa'.[9] It was on the latter that he now decided to concentrate.

The invasion of Abyssinia was undertaken primarily to demonstrate Italy's great-power status and, in doing so, avenge Adowa, the scene of the disastrous defeat of Italian troops in 1896. One of the more frustrating aspects of Versailles had been Italy's failure to acquire any new colonies and Mussolini now intended to recreate the glories of the Roman Empire and achieve a 'place in the sun' to rival Britain and France. Further motives were the prospect of economic gains in the form of oil, coal and gold and of African recruits for the Italian army. Mussolini also thought of East Africa as a fertile area for Italian settlement, given the expected increase in population from the 'Battle for Births'. Abyssinia was in any case the only remaining uncolonized African territory and seemed an easy target, given Italy's military superiority and its presence in neighbouring Eritrea and Somaliland.

Italy had sponsored Abyssinian entry to the League of Nations in 1923 and made a treaty of friendship with the Emperor Haile Selassie in 1928. But these actions belied Mussolini's real aims. The attack on Abyssinia had been under consideration at least from 1932 and possibly before, and a specific plan was devised in the summer of 1934. Timing was important since Mussolini was intent on conquering Abyssinia before German rearmament was complete, in order to have time to move Italian forces back to Europe to counter a possible further threat to Austria. As he wrote to Pietro Badoglio, the Chief of General Staff, on 30 December 1934,

> time is working against us. The longer we delay the solution of this problem, the more difficult the task will be. . . . One essential condition . . . is having a peaceful Europe on our hands, certainly for the period of two years 1935–36 and 1936–37.[10]

However, an excuse was needed for this act of aggression and, more importantly, an assurance that Britain and France would not intervene. A pretext was easily found when thirty Italians were killed in a clash with the Abyssinians at Wal Wal on the Somali–Abyssinia frontier in December 1934. Ensuring the compliance of the western powers was more difficult though Hitler's accession to power meant that Britain and France were now more dependent on Italian support to counteract any German moves. When in March 1935 Hitler announced rearmament the three powers convened a conference at the Italian lakeside town of Stresa. Here they formed the so-called Stresa Front, an anti-German agreement by which they undertook to act against any violation of peace treaties. Even before this, Mussolini believed he had secured French acquiescence in his plans since in January 1935 the French Foreign Minister, Pierre Laval, had agreed that France had no interests other than economic in Abyssinia, and had also given a verbal understanding that Italy might acquire political control of the country. While the French had not exactly agreed to a military take-over of Abyssinia, Mussolini felt fairly confident that they would not object.

Britain was harder to convince. At Stresa the subject of Abyssinia was raised informally but there was no agreement, though Mussolini took silence to mean consent. Then in June 1935 the British Foreign Secretary, Anthony Eden, visited Rome with a plan to allocate the Ogaden region of Abyssinia to Italy and compensate Abyssinia with access to the sea via British Somaliland. Mussolini rejected this offer, but it seemed to indicate that Britain was prepared to be accommodating. Further evidence of a conciliatory attitude was a British Foreign Office report in August 1935, a copy of which was acquired by Mussolini, which suggested that Britain had no interests in Abyssinia strong enough to justify resisting an Italian conquest.[11]

Mussolini thereupon launched his invasion in October 1935, looking forward to a quick victory, enhanced prestige and glory for the Italian army. His assessment of the British government's attitude was largely correct but he had reckoned without the popularity of the League of Nations and the impact on public opinion, given that a British general election was pending in November. When Haile Selassie appealed to the

League it imposed economic sanctions on Italy. This posed an insoluble dilemma for Britain, whose government wished to retain Italy's support in the already weakened Stresa Front but at the same time felt obliged to uphold the authority of the League as the guarantor of collective security.

League sanctions turned out to be half-hearted. There was no ban on exports to Italy of essential commodities such as coal, oil and steel and Britain refused to close the Suez Canal, a vital route for the transport of Italian troops and supplies to East Africa. Germany, Austria and Hungary ignored the sanctions, though Hitler was also secretly helping the Abyssinians, hoping to tie down Italy in a prolonged war. While sanctions scarcely impeded the Italian war effort they did succeed in mobilizing Italian public opinion behind Mussolini, whose popularity soared to new heights. Meanwhile, British and French ambiguity was revealed in the December 1935 Hoare–Laval Plan, which sought to give Italy much of Abyssinia in return for Abyssinian access to the sea, through the so-called 'corridor for camels'. This plan was leaked to the press before it could be implemented and, because it contradicted the previous policy of support for the League, had to be disowned. Sanctions continued through 1936 but the western powers were now more concerned with the implications of Hitler's occupation of the Rhineland than with Abyssinia.

By mid-1936, with the capture of the capital, Addis Ababa, the conquest of Abyssinia could be counted a success. Italian troops initially commanded by De Bono and then by Badoglio had used aerial bombing and poison gas to defeat Haile Selassie's ill-equipped army and in June 1936 Victor Emmanuel was proclaimed emperor.

But despite this outward triumph, Italy did not benefit from its conquest. The war had been a heavy military and financial burden costing 40 million lire and Italy's limited armaments had been depleted. Italian troops remained tied down in guerrilla conflict in Abyssinia for the next three years. Economic gains were negligible. Mussolini reached the peak of his popularity in Italy, but the war also confirmed his belief that an aggressive policy paid off and this encouraged him to embark on further risky and expensive enterprises such as intervention in the Spanish Civil War.

The effects of the war on European diplomacy were arguably more significant than its impact on Italy. Abyssinia was a turning point in European diplomatic relations. First, it destroyed the credibility of the League as a peacekeeping body. Already weakened by its ineffectiveness over Japan's invasion of Manchuria in 1931, the League was shown to be quite incapable of dealing with aggressors. The collapse of the

League in turn reinforced the view in France and, especially, Britain that appeasement of Hitler might be the only viable option. Second and more importantly, Abyssinia shifted the balance of power in Germany's favour. It left Mussolini at a 'diplomatic cross roads'.[12] Though sanctions had worsened relations with Britain and France he still had some room for manoeuvre, including the possibility of reviving the Stresa Front and thereby curbing Hitler's ambitions; but instead he made the fateful choice of friendship and eventual alliance with Germany. This decision seemed advantageous at the time. Mussolini could see that the western powers were unlikely to allow him to make the Mediterranean an 'Italian lake' or to acquire further territory, whereas it was clear that Hitler would not hinder Italian plans for expansion.

Therefore Abyssinia was followed by joint German–Italian involvement in Spain and by the Axis agreement. The break-up of the Stresa Front gave Hitler the opportunity to remilitarize the Rhineland in March 1936, and Britain and France were unable to prevent it. Mussolini dropped his opposition to the Anschluss, and in March 1938 acquiesced in the annexation of Austria to the Reich, which gave further significant strategic advantages to Germany.

It was not Italy but Germany which gained most from Abyssinia. The diplomatic consequences of Mussolini's African adventure greatly improved Hitler's chances of putting into practice his plans for eastward expansion. Unfortunately for Mussolini they also left him little option but to support these ambitions.

## Questions

1. Why, and with what results for Italian foreign policy, did Mussolini embark on the invasion of Abyssinia in October 1935?
2. With reference to the period 1922 to 1938, comment on the view that 'it was always a misjudgement to believe that Mussolini could make a valuable contribution to the maintenance of peace'.

# SOURCES

## 1. ITALY, GERMANY AND AUSTRIA, 1934–8

### Source A: Mussolini's view of Austria in 1934.

Austria is aware she can count on us for the defence of her independence as a sovereign state.

### Source B: Ciano reflects on the implications of Mussolini's visit to Berlin in September 1937.

Will the solidarity between the two regimes suffice to form a real bond of union between two peoples drawn in opposite directions by race, culture, religion and tastes? No one can accuse me of being hostile to the pro-German policy. I initiated it myself. But should we, I wonder, regard Germany as a goal, or rather as a field for manoeuvre? . . . We shall see. The Rome–Berlin Axis is today a formidable and extremely useful reality. I shall try to draw a line from Rome to Tokyo, and the system will be complete.

### Source C: A conversation between Mussolini and Joachim von Ribbentrop (then German ambassador to Britain) in November 1937.

Finally, Ribbentrop discusses the Austrian question. . . . The Duce replies that Austria is a German country by race, language and culture. The Austrian question must not be considered as a problem affecting Italy and Germany, but, on the contrary, as a problem of an international order. For his part . . . he is tired of mounting guard over Austrian independence, especially if the Austrians no longer want their independence.

### Source D: Ciano comments on events in Austria on 11 March 1938.

March 11. A hectic day for Austria. From hour to hour telephone messages have confirmed the mobilization on the Bavarian frontier and the German decision to attack. At midday Schuschnigg accepted the postponement of the plebiscite, but the Germans did not consider that enough and wanted him to resign . . . he asked us what he should do. I have conferred several times with the Duce. We cannot from here assume the responsibility of advising him one way or the other. . . . The French Chargé d'Affaires asked to come and see me, on instructions from Paris, in order to form a concerted plan for the Austrian situation. I replied that we have no intention of consulting with anybody. . . . After sanctions, the non-recognition of the Empire and all the other miseries inflicted on us since 1935, do they [Britain and France] expect to rebuild Stresa in an hour, with Hannibal at the gates? Thanks to their policy, France and England have lost Austria. For us too it is not an advantage. But in the meantime we have acquired Abyssinia.
6 p.m. Schuschnigg resigns and Seyss-Inquart takes his place. An independent Austria no longer exists.

**Source E: Mussolini comments on the Anschluss in a speech in the Chamber of Deputies on 16 March 1938.**

When an event is fated to take place, it's better it takes place with you rather than despite of, or worse still, against you.

## Questions

1. In the context of the Sources, explain the terms: 'Rome–Berlin Axis' (Source B), 'Stresa' (Source D). [4]
2. What does Ciano in Source B see as the advantages of Italian–German friendship? What reservations does he have about this policy? [4]
3. In what circumstances did Mussolini act to defend Austrian independence in 1934 (Source A)? [4]
4. Using the Sources and your own knowledge, explain why Mussolini's attitude to Austrian independence changed between 1934 and 1938. [7]
*5. What is there in the content of Sources C, D and E to suggest that Mussolini and Ciano were resigned to, rather than enthusiastic about, the German annexation of Austria? [6]

### Worked answer

*5. In Source C Mussolini concedes that Austria might become part of Germany, but he appears to be searching for reasons to justify his change of policy. He is trying to persuade himself that the Austrians don't want independence, which was not necessarily the case.

In Source D Ciano takes a neutral stand on the Anschluss in his reply to Schuschnigg's request for advice. However, he has clearly washed his hands of Austria and tries to lay the blame for the Anschluss on Britain and France on the grounds that these powers by their opposition to the conquest of Abyssinia have forfeited Italian friendship and thereby precluded any cooperation: 'Thanks to their policy, France and England have lost Austria.' He is, however, clearly unhappy about the Anschluss when he writes: 'For us too it is not an advantage.'

Finally Mussolini, speaking a few days after the Anschluss (Source E), indicates that he regards the union as inevitable and implies that he is acquiescing to it because he has no choice rather than out of positive support for Germany. He has to pretend approval in order not to reveal Italy's powerlessness or lose face.

These sources show that Mussolini and Ciano were unable to prevent the Anschluss, and in feigning neutrality or support were simply making the best of a bad job, as when Ciano consoles himself that Italy has at least acquired Abyssinia. There is an underlying unease about the impact of the Anschluss on the balance of power between Italy and Germany, and a distinct feeling that it was not to Italy's benefit.

# SOURCES

## 2. ITALIAN INTERVENTION IN THE SPANISH CIVIL WAR

### Source F: Mussolini explains the reasons for Italian intervention in Spain in November 1937.

First of all we have spent about four and a half milliards in Spain. German expenditure, according to what Goering said, is in the region of three and a half milliards. We wish to be paid and must be paid. But there is over and above that a political aspect. We want Nationalist Spain which has been saved by virtue of all manner of Italian and German aid to remain closely associated with our manoeuvres ... Rome and Berlin must therefore keep in close contact so as to act in such a way that Franco will always follow our policy ... Franco must come to understand that, even after our eventual evacuation, Majorca must remain an Italian base in the event of a war with France.

### Source G: The German ambassador to Italy comments on the advantages to Germany of Italy's involvement in Spain.

The role played by the Spanish conflict as regards Italy's relations with France and England could be similar to that of the Abyssinian conflict, bringing out clearly the actual, opposing interests of the powers, and thus preventing Italy from being drawn into the net of the Western powers and used for their machinations. The struggle for dominant political influence in Spain lays bare the natural opposition between Italy and France; at the same time the position of Italy as a power in the western Mediterranean comes into competition with that of Britain. All the more clearly will Italy recognize the advisability of confronting the Western powers shoulder to shoulder with Germany.

### Source H: A British newspaper account of the Italian role in the Battle of Guadalajara, March 1937.

Italy's Second 'Caporetto'

*Retreat goes on*

*Italians 'useless in Spain'*

Spanish Government troops continue to advance northeast of Madrid and the collapse of the Italian army is now fully confirmed. Vast quantities of equipment and munitions were thrown away or left behind. It is thought that the Italians have not suffered heavy losses as they appear in the main to have kept out of the reach of the Government troops. A special correspondent of the Press Association who has visited the front described it as a 'second Caporetto'. The correspondent says that the country is ideal for mechanized units, but the cold has destroyed the morale of the rebels. He says that the Italians are useless in such a climate.

### Source I: A historian explains Mussolini's decision to aid Franco.

The position of France was the key factor. Indeed, motivated by a determination to undermine French power, he had been infuriated by the news that Léon Blum, the French Prime Minister, planned to aid the Spanish Republic. . . . He saw the possibility of killing off for the foreseeable future the prospect that the Popular Front governments of Spain and France would be drawn together to the detriment of Italian ambitions in the Mediterranean. . . . A Nationalist victory might lead to the expulsion of the British from Gibraltar. It would probably give Italy access to bases in the Balearic Islands. In either eventuality it was an excellent opportunity to weaken Britain's communication with Suez.

### Questions

*1. Explain: 'Second Caporetto' (Source H), 'Popular Front governments' (Source I). [4]
2. How far do Sources F and I agree on Mussolini's motives for intervening in Spain? [5]
3. How had the 'Abyssinian conflict' brought out the 'opposing interests' of Italy and the western powers (Source G)? [5]
4. In what ways does Source G suggest that Germany was using Italian intervention in Spain for its own ends? [6]
5. How do Sources F and H suggest that Italian involvement in Spain may have been less than successful? [5]

**Worked answer**

*1. [This type of question requires a fairly brief answer but, since there are two marks for each part, you need to expand your definitions.]

'Second Caporetto' refers to the scene of Italy's crushing defeat by the Austrians in the Alps in 1917 during the First World War. This was a disaster for Italian troops with numerous casualties.

'Popular Front governments' refers to the coalitions of left-wing parties, including Socialists and Communists, which were in power in France and Spain in 1936. The setting up of such fronts, which entailed Communists working with other left-wing parties, was promoted by the Soviet Union from 1935 in order to counteract Fascism.

# 7

# 'A BRUTAL FRIENDSHIP'?

## The German alliance, war and Mussolini's downfall

### BACKGROUND NARRATIVE

As we saw in chapter 6, by 1938 Mussolini, whether for pragmatic or ideological reasons, had opted for friendship with Germany and, like his fellow dictator, he was making no secret of his expansionist aims. In a speech to the Grand Council in February 1939 he announced his determination to break out of the 'prison' of the Mediterranean, a course of action which would bring him into conflict with Britain and France. He declared that the bars of the prison were 'Corsica, Tunisia, Malta and Cyprus; its sentinels Gibraltar and Suez', and added: 'the tasks of Italian policy, which could not and does not have European territorial aims, save Albania, is in the first place to break the prison bars.'[1]

In April 1939 he sent Italian troops to occupy Albania and in May he and Hitler signed an alliance, the Pact of Steel, which committed Italy to support Germany in the event of war, even one started by the Germans. This was an increasingly probable scenario, but Mussolini had little intention of embarking on a major war in Hitler's interests in 1939. Such an undertaking was ruled out by Italy's military and economic unpreparedness. Mussolini was taken aback by Hitler's decision to invade Poland in August 1939, but he had no alternative but to remain neutral when the democracies declared war on Germany. He described the Italian position as non-belligerency (which sounded more positive than neutrality), but this was still very distasteful since it appeared weak and indecisive and contradicted his previous aggressive stand. It was also uncomfortably reminiscent of Italian neutrality, to which he had been vehemently opposed at the beginning of the First World War. Nevertheless, Mussolini tried to keep his options open, attempting unsuccessfully to persuade Britain to make peace in May 1940.

But when, following Hitler's successful invasion of France and the Low Countries in May and June 1940, it looked as though Germany was bound to triumph, Mussolini finally decided to join in the war despite the opposition of Ciano, Victor Emmanuel and most of the Italian public. He thought the conflict was as good as over and feared lest Italy be deprived of its share of the spoils. However, Italy made few territorial gains and, contrary to his expectations, the war was by no means won.

Mussolini had no wish to appear subservient to Hitler and at first tried to pursue a separate war whereby Italy would expand its own sphere of influence in the Balkans. Axis strategy in fact required German–Italian cooperation, for example to capture Malta, a British base which dominated the eastern Mediterranean, or to attack the British forces in North Africa. But Mussolini rejected collaboration with his ally and instead, to further his Balkan territorial ambitions, chose to invade Greece in October 1940. This was a total failure since Italian troops were soon in retreat and the situation had to be retrieved by German intervention in April 1941. In September 1940 the Italian army in Libya crossed the frontier into Egypt but by December it too had been driven back and early in 1941 the Germans had to take over the campaign in North Africa as well. Mussolini had embarked on too many ambitious enterprises for his limited resources.

The Italian campaign continued to be a catalogue of disasters. In November 1940 a British air attack destroyed half the Italian fleet at the southern naval base of Taranto; this was followed by another Italian naval defeat off Cape Matapan in March 1941. At the same time the Italians were also driven out of East Africa, destroying Mussolini's dream of a new Roman Empire. Mussolini then foolishly depleted his forces by sending Italian divisions to the Russian front. Finally, after some initial successes in North Africa where Rommel had taken command, the German–Italian army was defeated at El Alamein in November 1942 while an Anglo-American landing in French North

Africa ensured that it was only a matter of time before Italy itself was invaded. Sure enough, in July 1943 the Allies landed in Sicily.

These defeats sealed Mussolini's fate. The war had never been very popular and became considerably less so when news of military disasters filtered back. Mussolini had never been as absolute a dictator as he liked to think. He now had to contend with the King and with the Fascist Grand Council, which he had ignored for years. A momentous vote in the Grand Council on 24 July paved the way for the Duce's removal from power by the King the following day. Marshal Badoglio took over as Head of Government and on 8 September an armistice was signed. However, the consequent German occupation of the north and central parts of the country ensured that the war in Italy would continue for another eighteen months.

Following his deposition, Mussolini was imprisoned on the offshore islands of Ponza and La Maddalena and finally at Gran Sasso, a resort in the Apennines. It was from here that he was rescued and flown to Munich on 12 September in a daring exploit by German commandos led by Colonel Skorzeny. A few days later Hitler installed him as head of a puppet government on Lake Garda in northern Italy. Here in the Republic of Salò (named after the town where the government had its headquarters) Mussolini reverted to the social radicalism which had characterized early Fascism. The programme drawn up at the Congress of Verona in November 1943 was republican (resentment of Victor Emmanuel being a favourite theme of Mussolini's writings in exile), and called for nationalization of industry, workers' control of enterprises, and social reforms. In deference to Hitler it was also anti-Semitic and 9,000 Italian Jews were deported to death camps from the German-occupied areas. Mussolini was eager to take revenge on those who had plotted his deposition and following show trials, Ciano, De Bono and three other Fascists were executed in January 1944.

However, it was soon apparent that Mussolini had lost all vestiges of power. His attempts to conciliate workers and peasants were unconvincing and were easily negated by the Germans. He was unable to prevent Germany from taking over Italian territory in South Tyrol, Trieste and Fiume, making the Saló Republic into a police state and deporting hundreds of thousands of Italian workers to Germany for forced labour. Not surprisingly, most of the working population in the occupied area renewed their support for left-wing parties and many joined the Resistance.

By early 1945 time was running out for Mussolini as the Allies advanced into northern Italy. In April he tried to escape by joining a German unit moving north, but was discovered and killed by partisans on 28 April 1945.

## ANALYSIS (1): HOW FAR WAS MUSSOLINI ABLE TO FOLLOW AN INDEPENDENT FOREIGN POLICY BETWEEN 1939 AND 1943?

It was clear even in 1938 that Mussolini was very much the junior partner in his alliance with Hitler and his standing deteriorated further over the following five years. He was not consulted over the Anschluss though Hitler was very relieved when he passively accepted it. Mussolini's role as an arbitrator at Munich was illusory since the final agreement was wholly in Hitler's favour. Nor did Hitler inform him prior to occupying the remainder of Czechoslovakia in March 1939 – as Mussolini remarked, 'every time Hitler takes a country he sends me a message'.[2]

Mussolini was uneasily aware of his subservient role and of the fact that he had made a number of concessions to Hitler, allowing Germany to expand towards the Danube and the Balkans and up to the Italian frontier, without gaining anything in return. He was therefore determined to take the initiative and for this reason invaded Albania in April 1939, a largely unnecessary act of aggression since that country was already effectively under Italian control.

Shortly afterwards, the Pact of Steel was agreed by Ciano and Ribbentrop and signed by Mussolini on 12 May. This treaty committed both powers to support one another in the event of war but since in 1939 Germany was much more likely to initiate hostilities than Italy, it was to the latter's disadvantage. Various reasons have been put forward to explain why Mussolini agreed to this alliance which tied him to support German foreign policy aims. He possibly hoped to use it to get German backing for the pursuit of Italian interests in the Mediterranean and Africa, and he may even have thought it would prevent war by deterring the western powers from challenging Germany. Whatever the reason, he did not take the agreement very seriously and had no intention of going to war in 1939. Soon after signing the Pact he informed Hitler that he wanted to postpone any conflict till 1943 and in August he sent the Germans a long shopping list of Italy's military needs which there was no possibility of them providing. Hitler, too, was under no illusions about the Pact and had a low opinion both of Mussolini and of Italian military capacity.

Hoping against hope for a period of peace, Mussolini was dismayed when in August 1939 he learnt that Germany was preparing for an imminent attack on Poland. As Ciano noted in his diary, 'the fate that might befall us does not interest them in the least. They know that the decision will be forced by them rather than by us.'[3] The Duce was also wrong-footed by the Nazi–Soviet pact of 23 August, which he was only told about two days before it was signed.

Mussolini declined to enter the war in September 1939 but this was more from military weakness than prudence and he was eager not to be left out of what he believed would be an easy victory. When German forces swept through western Europe in May 1940, though predictably he was again not informed beforehand, Mussolini could wait no longer and on 10 June declared war on Britain and France. Given German success, his decision was probably inevitable. It was influenced by the prospect of territorial gains but also by fear of German dominance, jealousy of German achievements and awareness that victory would enable him to radicalize the regime and 'settle accounts with the Conservatives and Church'.[4] Mussolini was gratified that on the outbreak of war he was able to take command of the operational forces.

However, Italian troops had only advanced a few miles into the French Alps before a Franco-German armistice was signed on 25 June. Mussolini had to compete with the French Vichy government whose support Hitler wished to keep, and Italy therefore failed to make any acquisitions from France except Sardinia. That he did not obtain more was partly Mussolini's own fault. He apparently did not press his claims very strongly, demanding Nice and Corsica but not Tunisia which, with its port of Bizerta, would have been much more valuable in supplying Italian troops in Africa.

Mussolini was eager to follow an independent military strategy and tried to pursue what he called a 'parallel war' in the Balkans, attacking Greece on 28 October 1940, an enterprise undertaken partly to offset German intervention in Romania. But Italian troops were driven out of Greece within a week and had to fight a defensive war for the next three months. Eventually in April 1941 Germany came to their aid but the outcome was to extend German influence in the Balkans, which was exactly what Mussolini had wanted to prevent. He would have been better employed accepting German help in an attack on Malta to undermine British naval supremacy in the Mediterranean, followed by an attack on Egypt to capture Suez. But there were no concerted plans for this till later. Meanwhile, in North Africa, as in Albania, Italian troops were driven back before being rescued by German intervention in 1941. Henceforth it was Germany which dictated strategy.

Mussolini's dependence on Hitler resulted largely from Italy's military failings. Mussolini had little grasp of strategy. He wanted to make all the decisions himself and did not consult his generals, often giving them unrealistic objectives. He was alternately impulsive and irresolute, frequently changing his mind, as well as being hopelessly over-optimistic. However, the main problem was the poor state of the Italian armed forces. Mussolini had been deceived by his commanders and had deceived himself about their capacity. The period between 1935 and 1938 had seen substantial military expenditure, amounting to 11.8 per cent of national income compared with 12.9 per cent in Germany, 6.9 per cent in France and 5.5 per cent in Britain,[5] but there was little to show for this outlay as much was wasted or invested in inferior armaments. Mussolini boasted of an 'airforce capable of blotting out the sun'.[6] But in fact it had only 1,000 planes and no long-range bombers, while the main fighter aircraft, the Fiat CR42 biplane, was slow and ill-designed.[7]

Mussolini claimed an army of eight million but only 0.8 million men could be mobilized in 1939 and by 1940 the total was only three million, while many of the rifles and much of the artillery dated back to the First World War. There were also shortages of anti-aircraft and anti-tank guns and only 1,500 armoured cars (together with lack of aircraft, a serious deficiency in the North African campaign), while the navy possessed no aircraft carriers. Furthermore, the three services were reluctant to cooperate and except for the airforce were rooted in pre-1918 traditions.

Italy had always been short of natural resources and this shortage was greatly exacerbated during the war when trade with Britain and much of the rest of the world was cut off and Germany was Italy's only source of many vital raw materials. Oil was in particularly short supply, with Romania only able to provide half Italy's peacetime requirements, while shortages of coal and iron ore led to a fall in steel production of 20 per cent between 1940 and 1942. It therefore proved impossible to produce the necessary war materials – for example, only 2,400 aircraft were produced in 1942, the same number as in 1941.[8]

Where Italy did have military advantages, these were soon negated. It had more submarines than Britain but one-third were sunk in the first three weeks of the war. To gain more credibility with Hitler, Mussolini unwisely sent 200,000 troops to the Russian front in 1941, when they would clearly have been better used in the North African campaign. Likewise, the best artillery and anti-tank guns were sent to Russia rather than Libya.

By 1941 the parallel war policy had had to be abandoned and it was clear that far from being an asset to the German war machine, Italy was a burden. As German Minister of Propaganda Goebbels commented, 'we have the worst allies that could possibly be imagined'.[9] Mussolini had lost what little initiative he possessed and had no alternative but to follow 'tamely and fatalistically in Hitler's wake'.[10] For example, he joined the Führer in declaring war on the USSR in June 1941 and, though he was under no obligation to fight on Japan's behalf, he also followed Germany in declaring war on the United States in December of that year.

In addition to dominating war strategy, the Germans increasingly took over operations within Italy itself. The Luftwaffe arrived in Sicily in 1941 and German troops also established themselves on Italian territory. Further underlining Italy's inferior position, 350,000 Italian 'guest workers' were sent to Germany where they were used as forced labour. The Italians were uncomfortably aware of their second-class status; as Ciano commented in his diary in January 1942,'[Mussolini] has before him the transcript of a telephone call by one of Kesselring's [the German commander in Italy] allies, who speaking with Berlin called us "macaroni" and hoped that Italy too would become an occupied country.'[11] But it was impossible to reverse this subordination.

At meetings with Hitler Mussolini was regularly outmanoeuvred and Italian views ignored. Conferences between the two dictators were irregular, usually only held at moments of crisis; relying on an interpreter, Mussolini often did not understand all that was said. From 1942 the Italians pleaded with Hitler to seek a separate peace with the USSR in order to release troops for western Europe and North Africa, but he took no notice. At a meeting in Salzburg with Mussolini in April 1943 (the first for a year), he convinced the Duce that the war could still be won. At a final conference on 19 July at Feltre in northern Italy Mussolini failed to get German agreement to Italy's withdrawal from the war and left the meeting apparently persuaded by Hitler's assurances of resumed submarine warfare and an air attack on London with V1 flying bombs.

Mussolini's removal from power just a few days after this conference reflected the general resentment within Italy of its subordination to its ally. Italy had been quite unable to follow an independent foreign or military policy and had therefore been dragged down to defeat in Germany's wake. Understandably, the Duce, having been responsible for foreign and military policy, was blamed for this dependency. Mussolini's impotence was to be further underlined during his sojourn in the Salò Republic where it was clear that he was nothing more than a German pawn. In his last interview on 25 April 1945 with the Archbishop of Milan, a dejected Mussolini was forced to admit that the 'Germans have always treated us like slaves and in the end they have betrayed us'.[12]

## Questions

1. Why and by what stages did Fascist Italy become the firm ally of Nazi Germany?
2. 'Until 1939 Mussolini's foreign policy was successful; thereafter it was disastrous.' Examine the validity of this view.


## ANALYSIS (2): WHAT FACTORS MADE IT POSSIBLE FOR MUSSOLINI TO BE REMOVED FROM POWER IN JULY 1943?

Mussolini's removal can be explained by military failures, the economic problems caused by the war, the fact that his popularity was always tenuous and finally by the limitations which the King and the Grand Council were able to place upon his authority.

By 1943, 'the whole structure of the corporate state . . . was coming apart at the seams'.[13] There had never been much enthusiasm for the war and as it went on dissatisfaction increased. Prices rose as a result of printing money, real wages declined by 30 per cent and rationing was introduced. Food prices in particular rose from an index of 100 in 1940 to 172 in 1942.[14] In autumn 1940 pasta (a staple part of the diet in most of Italy) was rationed, then bread in 1941; the wheat harvest fell by 25 per cent as peasants were drafted into the army and consumption of food halved between 1939 and 1943. A thriving black market and bureaucratic inefficiency ensured that the gap in standards of living between the middle and working classes increased.[15]

The war did not unite Italians behind the government but had the reverse effect. As early as June 1941 police informants were reporting that Mussolini was being described as 'a man in decline', by February 1942 they were saying 'he's too old' and by August 1942 'he's finished'.[16]

The eruption of mass industrial unrest in March 1943 bore out these impressions when strikes occurred involving 130,000 workers in the war production factories in Turin, Milan and other northern cities. These strikes were ostensibly over wages and rations, but they were also widely believed to have political motives. The precarious standing of the regime was demonstrated when the authorities had difficulty restoring order and only a few arrests were made.

But though the anti-Fascist movement had revived, this was unlikely to bring Mussolini down. Combined action by the King and the Fascist Party itself, backed by the army and police, was required to achieve this.

The origins of a plot to overthrow Mussolini can be detected as early as November 1942 after the El Alamein defeat. It involved the King, the Duke d'Acquarone, Minister of the Royal Household, who acted as a contact with other groups and individuals, former Liberal politicians and leading figures in the police and army.[17] Victor Emmanuel had always resented Mussolini's erosion of royal power, especially the rights over the succession to the throne acquired by the Grand Council in 1928 and the undermining of his command of the armed forces at the beginning of the war. But, despite criticism of Mussolini in the Senate and the Vatican, the King was afraid to act alone. The Fascist Party had the best chance of deposing Mussolini without fear of repercussions and, by 1943, a number of leading Fascists, perceiving that the war was lost, were considering a coup. They included Ciano, who was increasingly looking to make peace with the Allies, and a sizeable proportion of the Grand Council. Mussolini had already made some misguided changes to the Fascist Party general secretariat and in February 1943 he also dismissed Ciano, Grandi (the Minister of Justice) and Bottai (Minister of Education). He himself took over as Foreign Minister. The move reflected Mussolini's wish to assert himself and remove those who he imagined were unpopular figures, but its effect was to make these leading Fascists more disaffected and more determined to remove him.

The allied invasion of Sicily on 9 and 10 July was the last straw. On 16 July Mussolini agreed to convene the Grand Council for the first time since 1939. On 19 and 20 July he met Hitler at Feltre but failed to impress on him Italy's need for peace and as usual was taken in by the Führer's rhetoric. Unfortunately for Mussolini, the Feltre meeting coincided with a bombing raid on Rome, which further reduced his credibility. On 22 July Victor Emmanuel issued provisional orders to the army and police for Mussolini's arrest but the King was prudently waiting for the Grand Council to make the first move.

The meeting of the Grand Council on the night of 24–25 July was a lengthy (lasting for ten hours) and confused affair. Grandi, backed by the moderate Fascists, proposed a motion advocating reactivating the powers of the King, the Grand Council, parliament and the corporations. It did not refer to Mussolini by name or to ending the war, though in fact Grandi's underlying motive was to establish a moderate Fascist government, which would eventually seek peace. Another member of the Council, Farinacci, who was on the extreme wing of the Fascist movement, proposed a very similar motion, but he and Scorza (the Party Secretary) wanted the opposite to Grandi, a closer alignment with Germany and continuation of the war.[18] In the end, after prolonged debate, Grandi's motion was carried by nineteen votes to seven.

Mussolini's performance at the meeting was lack-lustre and it is surprising that he did not act more decisively to defeat or negate Grandi's motion. He could conceivably have forbidden the meeting, rallied more support or arrested the conspirators immediately afterwards. Though the resolution was effectively a vote of no confidence he may have felt he could afford to ignore the Grand Council since it was only an advisory body. He might even have believed that the vote would enable him to put pressure on the Germans to agree to Italy's withdrawal from the war. Such was the ambiguity of the resolution that some members of the Grand Council may not have realized it was the prelude to Mussolini's deposition.[19]

Mussolini seems to have believed that he would be able to survive the vote but he had reckoned without the King. Grandi's motion gave Victor Emmanuel the opportunity he was seeking. When on the afternoon of 25 July an apparently unsuspecting Mussolini went to the royal palace for his usual audience, Victor Emmanuel wasted no time in dismissing him and announcing that Marshal Badoglio, the former Chief of the General Staff, would take his place.

Mussolini's downfall was in great contrast to the fate of Hitler, who despite disastrous military defeats survived till the last days of the war. The difference was Mussolini's essentially weak hold on power, which was not backed up by military support. It also reflected his failure to impress most Italians with any feelings of loyalty to his regime.

## Question

1.  How was Mussolini able to be removed from power so easily in July 1943?

# SOURCES

## 1. ITALY'S PREPAREDNESS FOR WAR IN 1940

### Source A: Ciano assesses Italy's military strength in April 1939.

April 29 1939. Council of Ministers. Some decisions are approved to increase the power of the armed forces. The Duce is very much dissatisfied with them, with the exception of the Navy. He feels and rightly so, that beyond appearances . . . there is little underneath. I think so too. I have no exact information as to the Army, but the many rumours which I hear are distinctly pessimistic. Also, some impressions which I formed on the occasion of the mobilization for the Albanian undertaking, which was after all a small mobilization, have increased my doubts. The military make great play with a lot of names. They multiply the number of divisions, but in reality these are so small that they scarcely have more than the strength of regiments. The ammunition depots are short of ammunition. Artillery is outmoded. Our anti-aircraft and anti-tank weapons are altogether lacking. . . . We will not talk about the question of the Air Force. Valle [Chief of Staff of the Airforce] states that there are 3,006 first-line planes, while the Navy information service says that there are only 982.

## Source B: Ciano explains to Ribbentrop (the German Foreign Minister) why Italy cannot enter the war in 1939.

Italy needs a period of peace for the following reasons:
. . .
(b) To complete the construction and reconditioning of the six battleships, which has already commenced.
(c) For the renewal of the whole of our medium and heavy caliber artillery.
(d) For the further development of a plan for autarky, by which any attempt at a blockade by the satiated democracies must be thwarted.

## Source C: Further evidence from Ciano about Italy's ill-preparedness for war.

The officers of the Italian Army are not qualified for the job, and our equipment is old and obsolete. To this must be added the state of mind of the Italians, which is distinctly anti-German. The peasants go into the Army cursing those 'damn Germans'.

## Source D: Ciano requests German military and economic aid.

Berlin is showering us with requests for the list of our needs. We convene at the Palazzo Venezia at ten o'clock with the chiefs of staff of the three armies. . . . Before entering the Duce's room I remind these comrades of their responsibility. They must tell the whole truth on the extent of our stocks and not do what is usually done, be criminally optimistic. . . . We go over the list. It's enough to kill a bull – if a bull could read it. I remain alone with the Duce and we prepare a message to Hitler. We explain to him why it is that our needs are so vast, and we conclude by saying that Italy absolutely cannot enter the war without such provisions. . . . Soon Hitler's reply arrives. They can give us only iron, coal and lumber. Only a few anti-aircraft batteries.

## Questions

1. Explain the 'Albanian undertaking' (Source A), 'autarky' (Source B). [4]

2. Why would Italian public opinion tend to be 'anti-German' (Source C) in 1939? [4]
*3. What evidence is there in Sources A and D that Italian military planning was disorganized? [4]
4. What can be deduced from these sources about Ciano's own views on Italian entry into the war? [6]
5. Use your own knowledge to explain why, despite being ill-prepared, Italy finally entered the war in June 1940. [7]

### Worked answer

*3. Source A indicates that neither Mussolini, nor Ciano nor anyone else in authority had any real idea of the true state of the armed forces in 1939. Ciano apparently has to rely on rumours and impressions to get any information. It is surprising that as Foreign Minister he has 'no exact information'. It is clear that Mussolini and his ministers are being deceived by the generals as to the number of divisions available. The different services also appear to be competing and at odds with one another, as evidenced in the conflicting figures for planes given by the airforce and the navy.

Likewise in Source D, the chiefs of staff have to be reminded to give an accurate picture of Italy's military supplies and not be 'criminally optimistic'. This indicates that Mussolini was regularly given inaccurate and exaggerated information as to the state of the army.

# SOURCES

## 2. MUSSOLINI'S FALL FROM POWER

### Source E: A German informant reports from Rome in May 1943.

In the event of a crisis the Duce had at his disposal about 150 bodyguards equipped with revolvers; the Militia, very badly led and ill-equipped, who will go as a faithful flock to the slaughter; the old Fascists who are hardly organized at all ... and a police force, which is inadequately armed ... and very badly paid. On the other side the King ... has at his orders the well organized, disciplined, and reasonably armed military police. And then the Army.... The Fleet and the Airforce would obey blindly from above. There was widespread passive resistance to any co-operation with the Axis.

## Source F: Grandi's resolution at the Grand Council meeting on 24–25 July 1943.

The Grand Council, meeting at this time of great hazard ... Having examined the internal and international situation and the political and military conduct of the war, it proclaims the duty of all Italians to defend at all costs the unity, independence and liberty of the motherland, the fruits of the sacrifice and labour of four generations ... and the life and future of the Italian people. ... It declares that ... the immediate restoration is necessary of all state functions, allotting to the King, the Grand Council, the Government, Parliament and the Corporations the tasks and responsibilities laid down by our statutory and constitutional laws.

It invites the Head of Government to request His Majesty the King – towards whom the heart of the nation turns with faith and confidence – that he may be pleased to assume, for the honour and the salvation of the nation, together with the effective command of the armed forces, on land, sea, and in the air ... that supreme initiative of decision which our institutions attribute to him, and which, in all our national history, has always been the glorious heritage of our august dynasty of Savoy.

## Source G: Luigi Federzoni (a leading anti-Mussolini Fascist) comments on the Grand Council meeting (notes published in 1967).

Many people have asked what exactly we hoped to achieve by our initiative. The answer is very simple; one aim only: to secure as quickly as possible Italy's release from the German alliance and from the war. By then we knew that Mussolini was incapable of doing this; it was therefore necessary to force him to leave so that the country would not suffer a complete disaster. ... It was clear that the King himself needed some formal motive, some constitutional excuse; and, most important of all, only the Grand Council, because it was a Fascist institution, would be able to neutralize, as in fact it did, any possible revolt by the party and the militia in support of Mussolini.

## Source H: Victor Emmanuel dismisses Mussolini on 25 July 1943 (as described by Mussolini when in exile in the Salò Republic).

The King said, clipping his words, 'my dear Duce, it's no longer any good. Italy has gone to bits. Army morale is at rock bottom. The soldiers don't want to fight any more ... The Grand Council's vote is terrific – nineteen votes for Grandi's motion. ... You can certainly be under no illusion as to Italy's feelings with regard to yourself. At this moment you are the most hated man in Italy. ... You have one friend left and I am he. That is why I tell you that you need have no fears for your personal safety, for which I will ensure protection. I have been thinking the man for the job now is Marshal Badoglio. He will start by forming a government of experts for purely administrative purposes and for the continuation of the war. In six months' time we shall see. All Rome already knows about the Grand Council's resolution, and they are all expecting a change.'

## Questions

1. Define 'the old Fascists' (Source E). [2]
2. What do Sources E and H reveal of the weakness of Mussolini's position in 1943? [6]
3. Using the Sources and your own knowledge, explain why Mussolini might feel that he had little to fear from the text of Grandi's resolution in Source F? [6]
4. With reference to content and language assess with what skill Victor Emmanuel in Source H effects Mussolini's removal from power? [5]
*5. How reliable as evidence for the historian of events in 1943 are Sources E and G? [6]

## Worked answer

*5. *[In evidence questions remember that you need to look at the author of the Source, the purpose, when it was written and whether the Source is corroborated by other material.]*

Source E is information from a German – most likely connected with the German embassy – in Rome. This source is detailed and precise in its assessment of the balance of forces. The writer correctly deduces that Mussolini does not have any effective forces at his command and that the armed forces for the most part would obey the King. He also correctly evaluates public opinion as being hostile to Germany. These deductions are factual and objective and were borne out by events after the Grand Council meeting when the King had no difficulty in deposing Mussolini.

This informant was on the spot, possibly in contact with German intelligence and therefore in a good position to make valid observations. As the informant is reporting back to Berlin he has every incentive to convey accurate and up-to-date information. However, his views would have to be treated with some caution, since he was an outsider and not necessarily in a position to know all the facts.

Federzoni, writing in 1967 when Mussolini was clearly discredited, was obviously eager to portray his actions at the Grand Council meeting in the most favourable and anti-Mussolini light. Ending the war was one of the motives for removing Mussolini, but not necessarily the only one.

Many leading Fascists resented him by July 1943 on account of his ministerial changes and his ineptitude. There was no mention of making peace at the Grand Council meeting, though this was an underlying motive of some of the conspirators. Marshal Badoglio did not seek an armistice till September 1943. Inevitably after a twenty-year gap, Federzoni's recollections were somewhat selective. However, he was correct in reporting that only the Grand Council could 'neutralize' Mussolini and provide the King with a pretext. But a historian would require additional evidence in accounts by other Grand Council members present on 24–25 July.

# 8

# FASCISM AND NAZISM

## BACKGROUND NARRATIVE

When writing about Fascism, historians have to deal with a number of complex theoretical issues. One of these is whether the term 'Fascism' is applicable only to Italy between the wars, or whether it can be used to describe a variety of other inter-war (and post-war) regimes and movements – in other words, whether generic Fascism is a valid concept. Fascism has sometimes been defined very broadly to include post-Second World War dictatorships such as Juan Peron's in Argentina and Augusto Pinochet's in Chile as well as more recent European neo-Fascist movements. However, most historians confine their studies to inter-war Europe and particularly to Italy and Germany, the only two countries where genuine Fascist or Nazi movements came to power. In order to avoid using the term 'Fascism' too loosely, historians also have to distinguish between Fascist states and other right-wing authoritarian regimes. To do so, they must decide what, if any, are the defining characteristics or common denominators of Fascism, and indeed whether Fascism deserves to be described as an ideology at all.

Despite these difficulties, there have been several attempts to define Fascism, ranging from a single sentence – 'Fascism equals nationalism plus socialism' – to more elaborate definitions. Exponents of the concept of generic Fascism differ in approach and emphasis, but they all consider its main characteristics to be extreme nationalism, the predominance of the state over the individual, social radicalism, the development of a new political culture intended to create national unity, and the creation of a distinct political style.

In the inter-war period there were several movements which fit most of the above criteria. They include Szalasi's Arrow Cross Party in Hungary in the 1930s, the Fascist Iron Guard in Romania and Oswald Mosley's British Union of Fascists. However, none of these parties gained power and indeed the Hungarian and Romanian Fascists were suppressed by the more conventional right-wing regimes which took over in these countries.[1] Dictatorships were established in several other European states in the 1920s and 1930s, for example those of Metaxas in Greece and Pilsudski in Poland, but they are not usually regarded by historians as Fascist, and many, like Dollfuss in Austria between 1933 and 1934, Admiral Horthy in Hungary in the 1920s, Franco in Spain and Salazar in Portugal, were based more on right-wing conservatism and Catholicism rather than on a new ideology.

## ANALYSIS (1): HOW HAVE HISTORIANS DEFINED FASCISM?

Mussolini's most comprehensive definition of Fascism was expounded in 1932 in 'The Doctrine of Fascism', an article in the *Enciclopedia italiana*. Much of the language was obscure and mystical and he tended to dwell on what Fascism was against rather than what it was for; but he did eventually identify its most distinctive belief as the dominant role of the state: 'Fascism conceives of the state as an absolute, in comparison with which all individuals or groups are relative, only to be conceived of in their relation to the state.'[2] Mussolini therefore defined Fascism as totalitarian while also conveying the idea that it was a new beginning, a rebirth and revival of the Italian nation.

However, many historians dispute that Fascism (including Italian Fascism) can be regarded as an ideology at all. The historiography of Fascism, developing since the 1950s, has been influenced by the changing political landscape both within Italy and in the world at large. For example in the 1950s and 1960s Cold War period it was usual to depict Hitler and even Mussolini as essentially little different from Stalin. All three were regarded as totalitarian dictators with expansionist ambitions; thus Fascism and communism could be seen as two sides of the same coin, both equally reprehensible. From another perspective, Marxists from the 1930s onwards interpreted Fascism as an extreme form of counter-revolutionary capitalism directed against the working class in the interests of big business. Both these theories are now largely discounted. It is accepted that despite some similarities, Fascism can be clearly differentiated in aims and practice from communism. As far as the Marxist model is concerned, links between Fascism and the owners of industry have been proved to be more complex and tenuous than once imagined.

Examination of Fascism as a distinct set of political theories began in the 1960s with the work of the German writer Nolte.[3] In the ensuing decades, the main lines of controversy were drawn between historians who claimed that Fascism possessed a recognizably coherent set of values and those who considered that it was too contradictory and nebulous to qualify as an ideology at all. This in turn raised questions about the nature of Italian Fascism and particularly whether Mussolini, as the first Fascist leader, possessed a consistent ideology or whether he is more accurately described as a pragmatic opportunist, seeking power for its own sake.

One historian of Fascism, Stanley Payne,[4] describes Fascism as 'a form of revolutionary ultra-nationalism for national re-birth',[5] implying that Fascism was essentially seeking radical changes in the structure of society as well as promoting national or racial identity. He goes on to say that Fascist movements were distinctive in their ability to mobilize mass support and in relying on strong leadership figures – the *Führer-prinzip* or leadership principle. Another historian, F.L. Carsten,[6] considers the basic components of Fascism to be nationalism, anti-Semitism and mass appeal across social classes, its objective the establishment of an authoritarian and elitist state headed by a supreme leader.

Roger Eatwell[7] claims that although 'Fascist movements and regimes were characterized more by what they were against than what they were for', and can be 'defined essentially by . . . style and negations', nevertheless Fascism was an ideology in its own right, postulating a new and radical third way between capitalism and communism. Social radicalism was an indispensable ingredient of Fascism, so that Italy and Germany can be described as Fascist but Franco's Spain cannot. Eatwell sees Mussolini as having strong ideological motives, hence his reversion to extreme Fascism in the Salò Republic.[8]

Roger Griffin,[9] a leading exponent of the concept of generic Fascism, claims that the term 'Fascism' can also be applied to regimes and movements outside Europe and post-Second World War. He considers the common denominator to be a 'core myth' of national regeneration and rebirth. Like Eatwell, he sees Fascism as essentially radical and modernizing, striving to create a new order and a 'new man', and as fundamentally anti-conservative, though Fascists were obliged to collude with conservative forces in order to achieve power. He also claims that Mussolini, despite his often contradictory policies and tactics, 'stayed remarkably faithful to a single core myth, that of the creation of a new Italy based on a regenerated national community'; but he admits that 'the new Italy ultimately remained little more than myth'.[10]

Other historians dispute these views, however, arguing that to reduce Fascism to little more than a myth calls into question its ideological credentials. Even the proponents of generic Fascism agree that in Mussolini's Italy style was more important than policy or practice. Italian Fascism was notable for its emphasis on action, dynamism, youth and the cult of the Duce, and relied heavily on symbolism and ceremonial events. Propaganda was all-important and concepts such as totalitarianism and the corporate state were destined to remain mostly just propaganda.

As we have seen in chapter 1, though many of the ideas associated with Fascism were present in Italy and other parts of Europe before the First World War, they were the preserve of disparate individuals and minority movements. Attempts to portray Mussolini as a serious ideologue throughout his Socialist and Fascist periods do not seem very convincing. As described in chapter 2, early Fascism was largely an irrational, violent and negative movement and Mussolini's definition outlined at the beginning of this section was formulated some years after he came to power. Early Fascism did have some 'core' beliefs, notably nationalism and the promotion of authoritarian leadership, but these may not in themselves be sufficient to distinguish it from other right-wing movements. Also, Italian Fascism was not particularly racist, still less anti-Semitic (which clearly differentiates it from Nazism).

Totalitarianism made little impact in practice and Mussolini largely failed in his ambition to transform the lives of Italians. Just as historians dispute the radicalism of Italian Fascism, so they also regard it as incapable, except superficially, of generating mass support, alleging that while it had a wider appeal than most other parties, its most committed long-term adherents were from the middle and lower middle class.

Rather than a serious thinker, Mussolini is more often portrayed as a chameleon, adapting with some success to varying circumstances. Italian historians such as Renzo De Felice, who has completed a detailed multi-volume biography of the dictator, have been influenced by the Fascist heritage and its impact on post-1945 Italian politics. They are more inclined than non-Italian writers to ascribe an ideology to Mussolini. But other biographers of Mussolini such as Denis Mack Smith and R.J.B. Bosworth consider him to be a 'sawdust Caesar' deceived by his own propaganda, and question whether his regime had any real ideological content. As the Italian historian Gaetano Salvemini put it, searching for a genuine Fascist ideology may be as hard as 'looking in a dark room for a black cat which is not there'.[11]

## Question

1. To what extent did Mussolini succeed in putting his totalitarian theories into practice in Italy in the period 1925 to 1939?

## ANALYSIS (2): HOW DOES MUSSOLINI'S REGIME COMPARE WITH THOSE OF HITLER AND FRANCO?

In a speech made during his visit to Berlin in September 1937 Mussolini asserted that 'Fascism and Nazism are two manifestations of the parallel historical situations which link the life of our nations'.[12] It is certainly very easy to find similarities between Fascism and Nazism. Both emerged from the traumatic impact of the First World War and the economic and social crisis of the early 1920s. Hitler and Mussolini both began political life as outsiders from a lower social background, with left-wing programmes which they later modified in order to gain power. Both set up paramilitary organizations, were strongly anti-left and made no secret of their contempt for democracy and representative institutions. Mussolini, coming to power in 1922, was for many years indisputably the senior dictator and Hitler did not succeed till more than a decade later, having learnt from his example; the failed Munich Putsch of 1923 was modelled on the Fascist march on Rome in the previous year; like Mussolini, Hitler saw the value of utilizing the twin tactics of violence and legality.

Both dictators attracted support through propaganda and the emotional impact of mass rallies and ceremonies. To a great extent they appealed to a similar constituency of disgruntled ex-soldiers and disaffected middle-class groups. After little initial success, both achieved power by a mixture of electoral tactics and intimidation, by diverse appeals to different interests and with the backing of conservative groups. Hitler had more time to build up his power base in the 1920s and, especially, during the depression, and so was in a much stronger electoral position by 1933 than Mussolini had been in 1922. He was therefore able to establish complete control much more quickly.

Once in power, both set about banning opposition parties though the Gestapo and SS were undoubtedly far more ruthless and feared than the OVRA. A German writer's recollection of a rail journey in Italy in 1936 illustrates this difference between the two regimes:

the people in my compartment were telling anti-Mussolini jokes. The *carabiniere* of course walked up and down the train corridor and I, coming from a German ambience, was terrified. But what happened in the end was that the *carabiniere* came into the compartment, not to arrest us, but to tell other Mussolini jokes. . . . Such an episode could never have happened in Germany.[13]

Both regimes aspired to be totalitarian, with an overlap of state and party structures, but the results were mixed though Hitler was more successful in imposing a social transformation than was Mussolini. Both were aware of the importance of indoctrinating the younger generation, and both had similar social and demographic policies. Economic policies were also comparable, being a mixture of private enterprise and state control, with an emphasis on self-sufficiency. Equally, the two dictators both found it essential to bolster their popularity by means of a personality cult.

So far, any differences between the two regimes can be ascribed to national characteristics. For instance, it can be claimed that Hitler was more successful in imposing Nazi rule and norms because Germany was historically a more regimented society with more of a tradition of state control than Italy. Hitler was certainly the more powerful, and there were few curbs on his authority after the death of the President Hindenburg in 1934. Mussolini on the other hand had to contend with the existence of both the monarchy and the Church. In respect of the latter Mussolini was disadvantaged by the location of the Vatican on his doorstep and the influence of Catholicism as the only religion of significance in Italy. In Germany on the other hand, Hitler benefited from the weaker position of the Catholic Church and from the divisions between Catholics and Protestants. More importantly, Mussolini never succeeded in neutralizing the monarchy, the instrument of his eventual downfall; nor, unlike Hitler, did he ever establish control over or win the loyalty of the armed forces. The Nazi Party too, with its various agencies, was much more powerful and autonomous than the Fascist Party was allowed to become in Italy. Nazi domination in Germany intensified during the war and Hitler maintained his hold even when it was clear that Germany was losing; in Italy the reverse occurred, with Fascist influence diminishing with every successive defeat.

However, in crucial respects, notably on racism, anti-Semitism and avowed expansionism, the ideologies of Fascism and Nazism were quite different. For one thing, Hitler took ideas much more seriously than Mussolini and had a programme for racially motivated eastwards expansion worked out in his autobiography *Mein Kampf* in 1924, several years before he came to power. Racial theories permeated Nazi ideology and were its driving force, whereas Mussolini only belatedly adopted an anti-Semitic policy in 1938, though the limited nature of anti-Semitism in Italy can be explained by the fact that Jews were a less numerous and less noticeable section of the population than in Germany. Hitler had explicit foreign policy aims to dominate Europe and acquire living space for Germans, but though Mussolini frequently extolled war, Italian expansionism was never on the German scale. It has been argued, for example, that the Abyssinian war was more in keeping with nineteenth-century colonialism than with Nazi racial conflict.[14] And while Mussolini was not averse to using the German alliance as a means to pursue Italian hegemony in the Mediterranean and the Balkans (in any case a long-standing Italian foreign policy aim), he never envisaged involvement in a racial war of European conquest and domination. In these crucial respects therefore, Fascism and Nazism can be viewed as quite distinct ideologies.

Franco's regime in Spain is often linked with those of Mussolini and Hitler in a trio of European inter-war dictatorships. Franco's state is certainly more comparable with Italy than with Germany, and as we have seen in chapter 6, he received substantial, though not uncritical, support from Mussolini during the Civil War. Some historians argue that Spain under Franco was essentially Fascist in its suppression of the left and its authoritarian system, but most conclude that Franco had established an old-style military dictatorship rather than a Fascist one.

The Spanish dictator was anti-socialist and anti-democratic, and he adopted some of the trappings of Italian Fascism such as corporations, a Labour Charter and a youth movement. But Franco was a soldier, not a politician.[15] He owed his rise to power to the army, not to the Fascist Falange, which was only one element in his coalition and not the most important one. The Falange was created independently of Franco but he used it for his own ends before reducing it to a minor role. In the same way, his fellow military dictator in Portugal, Salazar, though he set up a one-party state in the early 1930s with some gestures to corporatism, outlawed the Fascist blueshirted United Syndicalists.

In Franco's Spain, the army and the Church were more powerful forces than the Falange. Franco was a genuine supporter of the Catholic Church, unlike Mussolini and Hitler who found it expedient to come to terms with the Church while secretly seeking to undermine it. Unlike Mussolini, Franco made few efforts to intervene in economic or social life or to try to engineer a social revolution. Francoism found its inspiration not in the future but in the past, in the imperial Spain of the sixteenth-century conquistadors, though there are also elements of this in Mussolini's nostalgia for the glories of the Roman Empire. There was no anti-Semitism in Spain, though this can be ascribed to the fact that Jews had been driven out several centuries before.

Franco was not a particularly charismatic leader, though a cult of the Caudillo grew up around him. Though a nationalist, he was too cautious to embark on war, even without the constraints of economic backwardness. His ideological support for Hitler during the war may argue in favour of an affinity between Franco and Fascism. He did not, however, go so far as to enter the conflict, though possibly more by good luck than good management. Views of Franco's regime are of course coloured by the fact that unlike his fellow dictators (except for Salazar), he survived till 1975, modifying his regime and therefore appearing less 'Fascist' with the passage of time.

Italy, Germany and Spain can therefore be seen in some key respects as distinct regimes. However, determining how much affinity there is between them depends very much on how Fascism is defined and on this issue the historical debate is still open.

### Question

1. Were the differences between the regimes of Mussolini and Hitler greater than the similarities?

## SOURCES

### MUSSOLINI AND ANTI-SEMITISM

### Source A: Mussolini's defence of racial policies, September 1938.

With respect to domestic affairs, the burning question of the moment is the racial problem. Those who try to make out that we have simply imitated or worse, that we have been obedient to suggestions, are poor fools whom we do not know whether to pity or despise. The racial problem has not broken out suddenly. . . . It is related to our conquest of our Empire; for history teaches that empires are won by arms but held by prestige. And prestige demands a clear-cut racial consciousness which is based not only difference but on the most definite superiority. The Jewish problem is thus merely one aspect of this phenomenon. . . . In spite of our policy, world Jewry for the last sixteen years has been an irreconcilable enemy of Fascism. . . . Nevertheless, Jews possessing Italian citizenship who have attained indisputable military or civil merits . . . will find understanding and justice.

### Source B: An Italian lawyer justifies the racial legislation (from an article written in December 1941).

Italy has the glory and privilege of constituting a race with its own biophysical structure, its own purity passed down by tradition. It has the glory of having its own race chosen by God, who is worshipped within the Catholic faith of which it is the seat. It takes pride in being an inextinguishable civilization, in having been the beacon of the Mediterranean, and now, under the aegis of Fascism, in resuming its path and its mission to establish a higher justice among peoples. These are the contents and the significance of the racial legislation, whose necessity Mussolini was again the first to recognize.

### Source C: An historian explains Mussolini's anti-Semitism.

There had always been an element in his thought, which saw the struggle between superior and inferior cultures as the motor of history. The acquisition of a new empire in Ethiopia increased this tendency to distinguish between peoples in a hierarchical way. . . . By the late 1930s Mussolini launched a second revolution, to give Fascism a new lease of life. As he was by this time falling increasingly under Hitler's influence, he almost certainly saw anti-semitism as a major factor in regenerating Fascist radicalism – in separating the men from the time-servers and opportunists who now made up much of the party.

### Source D: A different historical interpretation.

Subsequently he [Mussolini] tried to excuse himself by accusing the Germans of exerting pressure to push him into a racialist policy, but it is hard to discover evidence of any such pressure; the motive was rather his own spontaneous decision to show solidarity with Nazism and provide a convenient scapegoat for the years of austerity that he meant to impose on Italy.

### Source E: Another historical viewpoint.

To absolve Mussolini from any responsibility for the Holocaust . . . is absurd. To understand him as a philosophically convinced anti-Semite or any form of racist is equally implausible . . . Fascist racism was more opportunist and short-term than fanatical. It was as hollow as were many other aspects of Mussolinian administration.

### Questions

1. Define 'second revolution' (Source C) and 'Holocaust' (Source E). [4]
*2. Why was Mussolini in Source A eager to claim that his policies had not been 'simply imitated'? [4]

3. How does the writer in Source B endeavour to justify Italian racism? [4]
4. In what ways could Italian racist policy be said to be linked to the 'conquest of Empire' (Source A)? [5]
5. How far do you agree with the interpretations in these Sources of the reasons for Mussolini's racist and anti-Semitic policies? Use all the Sources and your own knowledge. [8]

## Worked answer

*2. Mussolini was eager to prove that he had not imitated Hitler. This was especially important in 1938 when he was fast moving to an alliance with Germany which was far from popular in Italy. The Anschluss in March 1938 had already illustrated Italian subservience to German aims and Mussolini was desperate to retain some parity with the previously inferior German dictator. He was already being accused of slavishly following Germany, which many Italians disliked. Introducing a racial policy would only too easily be seen as copying Germany, since there were few prior manifestations of it in Mussolini's Fascist writings, and it had suddenly materialized in 1938. Also, Jews comprised less than 1 per cent of the Italian population and some were members of the Fascist Party. There was only a limited amount of anti-Semitism in Italy, so the policy seemed even stranger. Mussolini therefore felt obliged to link it to indigenous Italian developments: the Abyssinian war, which had undoubtedly promoted latent racialism, seemed a good reason.

# NOTES

## 1. LIBERAL ITALY AND THE ORIGINS OF FASCISM

1 M. Blinkhorn: *Mussolini and Fascist Italy* (London: Methuen, 1984), p. 3.
2 A. Cassels: *Fascist Italy* (London: Routledge, 1977), p. 19.
3 Blinkhorn: op. cit., p. 13.
4 J. Pollard: *The Fascist Experience in Italy* (London: Routledge, 1998), p. 2.
5 P. Morgan: *Italian Fascism 1919–1945* (Basingstoke: Macmillan, 1995), p. 5.
6 Cassels: op. cit., p. 4.
7 R. Pearce: *Fascism and Nazism* (London: Hodder & Stoughton, 1997), p. 27.
8 A. Lyttelton (ed.): *Italian Fascisms from Pareto to Gentile* (London: Jonathan Cape, 1973), p. 24.
9 M. Clark: *Modern Italy* (London: Longman, 1984), p. 176.
10 J. Whittam: *Fascist Italy* (Manchester: Manchester University Press, 1995), p. 149.
11 Clark: op. cit., p. 150.
12 Pearce: op. cit., p. 25.
13 R. Thurlow: *Fascism* (Cambridge: Cambridge University Press, 1999), pp. 14–15.
Source A: Quoted in Pollard: op. cit., pp. 3–4.
Source B: Quoted in C. Seton-Watson: *Italy from Liberalism to Fascism 1870–1925* (London: Methuen, 1967), p. 390.
Source C: E.R. Tannenbaum: *Fascism in Italy – Society and Culture 1922–45* (London: Allen Lane, 1972), pp. 15–16.
Source D: Quoted in Lyttelton: op. cit., pp. 146–8.
Source E: Adapted from M. Robson: *Italy: Liberalism and Fascism 1870–1945* (London: Hodder & Stoughton, 1992), p. 37, and Pollard: op. cit., pp. 6–7.

## 2. THE RISE OF FASCISM: ITALY FROM 1919 TO 1922

1   J. Pollard: *The Fascist Experience* (London: Routledge, 1998), p. 39.
2   Ibid: p. 34.
3   Ibid: p. 28.
4   A. Cassels: *Fascist Italy* (London: Routledge, 1977), p. 27.
5   M. Blinkhorn: *Mussolini and Fascist Italy* (London: Methuen, 1984), p. 14.
6   C.F. Delzell (ed.): *Mediterranean Fascism* (New York: Harper & Row, 1970), p. 97.
7   Ibid: p. 98.
8   Quoted in R.J.B. Bosworth: *The Italian Dictatorship. Problems and Perspectives in the Interpretation of Mussolini and Fascism* (London: Arnold, 1998), p. 41.
9   R.J.B. Bosworth: *Mussolini* (London: Arnold, 2002), p. 153.
10  Cassels: op. cit., p. 37.
11  Blinkhorn: op. cit., p. 16.
Source A: J. Whittam: *Fascist Italy* (Manchester: Manchester University Press, 1995), pp. 145–6.
Source B: Delzell: op. cit., pp. 22–4.
Source C: Ibid, p. 37.
Source D: V. Mallia-Milanes: *The Origins of the Second World War* (Basingstoke: Macmillan, 1987), p. 21.
Source E: Quoted in A. Lyttelton: *Italian Fascisms from Pareto to Gentile* (London: Jonathan Cape, 1973), pp. 45–6.
Source F: Bosworth: op. cit., 2002, p. 168.
Source G: Whittam: op. cit., p. 39.
Source H: D. Mack Smith: *Italy and its Monarchy* (New Haven: Yale University Press, 1989), p. 249–50.
Source I: A. Lyttelton: *The Seizure of Power: Fascism in Italy 1919–1929* (London: Weidenfeld & Nicolson, 1973), p. 91.

## 3. FROM PRIME MINISTER TO DICTATOR, 1922 TO 1926

1   D. Mack Smith: *Mussolini* (London: Phoenix Press, 1998), p. 77.
2   F.L. Carsten: *The Rise of Fascism* (London: Batsford, 1982), p. 69.
3   J. Whittam: *Fascist Italy* (Manchester: Manchester University Press, 1995), pp. 49–50.
4   C.F. Delzell: *Mediterranean Fascism 1919–1945* (New York: Harper & Row, 1970), p. 54.
5   Whittam: op. cit., p. 41.
6   M. Whittock: *Mussolini in Power* (London: Collins Educational, 1998), p. 5.

7   A. Lyttelton: *The Seizure of Power: Fascism in Italy 1919–1929* (London: Weidenfeld & Nicolson, 1973), p. 111.

8   Ibid: pp. 108–9.

9   J. Pollard: 'Conservative Catholics and Italian Fascism', in M. Blinkhorn (ed.): *Fascists and Conservatives: the Radical Right and the Establishment in 20th Century Europe* (London: Unwin Hyman, 1990), p. 36.

10  Ibid: p. 132.

11  Mack Smith: op. cit., p. 69.

12  A. Cassels: *Fascist Italy* (London: Routledge, 1977), p. 48.

13  Whittam: op. cit., p. 50.

14  Lyttelton: op. cit., p. 271.

Source A: Quoted in ibid: p. 253.

Source B: Quoted in C. Seton-Watson: *Italy from Liberalism to Fascism 1870–1925* (London: Methuen, 1967), p. 654.

Source C: Quoted in J. Pollard: *The Fascist Experience in Italy* (London: Routledge, 1998), pp. 51–2.

Source D: Quoted in V. Mallia-Milanes: *The Origins of the Second World War* (London: Macmillan, 1987), p. 63.

Source E: Quoted in R. Klibansky (ed.): *Mussolini Memoirs 1942–1943* (London: Phoenix Press, 2000), pp. 158–9.

Source F: R. Wolfson: *Years of Change, European History 1890–1945* (London: Hodder & Stoughton, 1978), p. 284.

Source G: Delzell: op. cit., pp. 67–9.

Source H: Quoted in Whittam: op. cit., p. 153.

Source I: Quoted in Mallia-Milanes: op. cit., p. 64.

## 4. A TOTALITARIAN REGIME? MUSSOLINI AND THE FASCIST STATE

1   J. Pollard: *The Fascist Experience in Italy* (London: Routledge, 1998), p. 58.

2   M. Robson: *Italy: Liberalism and Fascism, 1870–1945* (London: Hodder & Stoughton, 1992), p. 75.

3   D. Mack Smith: *Mussolini* (London: Phoenix Press, 1998), p. 126.

4   E.R. Tannenbaum: *Fascism in Italy – Society and Culture 1922–45* (London: Allen Lane, 1972), p. 265.

5   Mack Smith: op. cit., p. 163.

6   R. Sarti, 'Italian Fascism: Radical Politics and Conservative Goals', in M. Blinkhorn (ed.): *Fascists and Conservatives: the Radical Right and the Establishment in 20th Century Europe* (London: Unwin Hyman, 1990), p. 26.

7   Pollard: op. cit., p. 62.

8   A. Lyttelton: *The Seizure of Power: Fascism in Italy 1919–1929* (London: Weidenfeld & Nicolson, 1973), p. 302.

9   Tannenbaum: op. cit., p. 93.
10  M. Blinkhorn: *Mussolini and Fascist Italy* (London: Methuen, 1984), p. 21.
11  *Ciano's Diary 1937–1938* (introduced by M. Muggeridge) (London: Methuen, 1952), p. 119.
12  Quoted in R.J.B. Bosworth: *The Italian Dictatorship. Problems and Perspectives in the Interpretation of Mussolini and Fascism* (London: Arnold, 1998), p. 193.
13  V. De Grazia, 'Culture of Consent', quoted in Bosworth: op. cit., p. 148.
14  T. Abse, 'Italian Workers and Italian Fascism', in R. Bessel (ed.): *Fascist Italy and Nazi Germany: Comparison and Contrasts* (Cambridge: Cambridge University Press, 1996), p. 40.
15  Mack Smith: op. cit., p. 148.
16  Lyttelton: op. cit., p. 400.
17  Pollard: op. cit., p. 66.
18  R. Thurlow: *Fascism* (Cambridge: Cambridge University Press, 1999), p. 32.
19  J.Whittam: *Fascist Italy* (Manchester: Manchester University Press, 1995), p. 81.
20  Quoted in C.F. Delzell: *Mediterranean Fascism 1919–1945* (New York: Harper & Row, 1970), pp. 93–4.
21  Pollard: op. cit., p. 74.
22  Ibid: p. 120.
23  Quoted in ibid: p. 123.
24  Ibid: p. 124.
25  Quoted in ibid.
26  A. Cassels: *Fascist Italy* (London: Routledge, 1977), p. 55.
27  Delzell: op. cit., pp. 174–6.
28  A. Young, 'Mussolini: an Unprincipled Politician', *Modern History Review* 11, 4, April 2000, pp. 31–3.
29  Cassels: op. cit., p. 52.
Source A: From Thurlow: op. cit., p. 31.
Source B: From Robson: op. cit., p. 77.
Source C: Quoted in Tannenbaum: op. cit., p. 165.
Source D: Cassels: op.cit., p. 69.
Source E: Quoted in Pollard: op. cit., p. 71.
Source F: Delzell: op. cit., pp. 157–64.
Source G: Quoted in Pollard: op. cit., p. 92.
Source H: Quoted in Robson: op. cit., p. 104.
Source I: Ibid: p. 105.

## 5. TRANSFORMING ITALY: HOW SUCCESSFUL WERE FASCIST ECONOMIC AND SOCIAL POLICIES?

1   A. Lyttelton: *The Seizure of Power: Fascism in Italy 1919–1929* (London: Weidenfeld & Nicolson, 1973), p. 338.
2   M. Blinkhorn: *Mussolini and Fascist Italy* (London: Methuen, 1984), p. 26.
3   Lyttelton: op. cit., p. 411.
4   E. R. Tannenbaum: *Fascism in Italy: Society and Culture 1922–1945* (London: Allen Lane, 1972), p. 191.
5   M. Clark: *Modern Italy* (London: Longman, 1984), p. 276.
6   J. Pollard: *The Fascist Experience in Italy* (London: Routledge, 1998), p. 79.
7   M. Robson: *Italy: Liberalism and Fascism 1870–1945* (London: Hodder & Stoughton, 1992), p. 101.
8   Clark: op. cit., p. 269.
9   Pollard: op. cit., p. 79.
10  Tannenbaum: op. cit., p. 119.
11  Lyttelton: op. cit., pp. 359–60.
12  Clark: op. cit., p. 267.
13  Lyttelton: op. cit., p. 333.
14  R. Wolfson: *Years of Change: European History 1890–1945* (London: Hodder & Stoughton, 1978), p. 273.
15  Pollard: op. cit., p. 87.
16  Ibid: p. 83.
17  Clark: op. cit., p. 271.
18  M. Blinkhorn: *Fascists and Conservatives. The Radical Right and the Establishment in Twentieth Century Europe* (London: Unwin Hyman, 1990), p. 70.
19  A.J. De Grand: *Fascist Italy and Nazi Germany, The Fascist 'Style of Rule'* (London: Routledge, 1995), p. 66.
20  Clark: op. cit., p. 255.
21  Tannenbaum: op. cit., p. 203.
22  T. Abse, 'Italian Workers and Italian Fascism', in R. Bessel (ed.): *Fascist Italy and Nazi Germany: Comparisons and Contrasts* (Cambridge: Cambridge University Press, 1996), p. 51.
23  J. Whittam: *Fascist Italy* (Manchester: Manchester University Press, 1995), p. 73.
24  P.R. Willson, 'Women in Fascist Italy', in Bessel: op. cit., p. 86.
25  Ibid: p. 88.
26  Robson: op. cit., p. 110.
Source A: C.F. Delzell (ed.): *Mediterranean Fascism 1919–1945* (New York: Harper & Row, 1970), p. 122–3.
Source B: Pollard: op. cit., p. 83.
Source C: Tannenbaum: op. cit., p. 52.

Source D: Pollard: op. cit., p. 85.
Source E: Whittam: op. cit., p. 159.
Source F: Robson: op. cit., p. 108.
Source G: Tannenbaum: op. cit., p. 141.
Source H: Quoted in R. Griffin (ed.): *Fascism* (Oxford: Oxford University Press, 1995), pp. 67–8.
Source I: Tannenbaum: op. cit., pp. 138–9.
Source J: Abse, op. cit., pp. 49–50.


## 6. 'GREAT, RESPECTED AND FEARED': HOW SUCCESSFUL WAS MUSSOLINI'S FOREIGN POLICY FROM 1922 TO 1938?

1 C.F. Delzell (ed.): *Mediterranean Fascism, 1919–1945* (New York: Harper & Row, 1970), p. 185.
2 M. Clark: *Modern Italy* (London: Longman, 1984), p. 280.
3 J. Whittam: *Fascist Italy* (Manchester: Manchester University Press, 1995), p. 101.
4 C. Lowe and F. Marzari: *Italian Foreign Policy 1870–1940* (London: Routledge & Kegan Paul, 1975), p. 185.
5 R.J.B. Bosworth: *Mussolini* (London: Arnold, 2002), p. 245.
6 Ibid: p. 251.
7 Delzell: op. cit., p. 185.
8 D. Mack Smith: *Mussolini's Roman Empire* (Harmondsworth: Penguin Books, 1976), p. 63.
9 Delzell: op. cit., p. 189.
10 Quoted in J. Pollard: *The Fascist Experience in Italy* (London: Routledge, 1998), p. 94.
11 Whittam: op. cit., p. 111.
12 M. Blinkhorn: *Mussolini and Fascist Italy* (London: Methuen, 1984), p. 35.
Source A: Quoted in Delzell: op. cit., p. 187.
Source B: *Ciano's Diary 1937–1938* (introduced by M. Muggeridge) (London: Methuen, 1952), p. 16.
Source C: Quoted in Lowe and Marzari: op. cit., p. 408.
Source D: *Ciano's Diary*: op. cit., p. 87.
Source E: Quoted in Lowe and Marzari: op. cit., p. 291.
Source F: Quoted in P. Knight: *The Spanish Civil War* (Basingstoke: Macmillan, 1991), p. 42.
Source G: Quoted in V. Mallia-Milanes: *The Origins of the Second World War* (Basingstoke: Macmillan, 1987), pp. 105–6.
Source H: Quoted in Knight: op. cit., pp. 68–9.
Source I: P. Preston: *A Concise History of the Spanish Civil War* (London: Fontana Press, 1996), p. 112.

## 7. 'A BRUTAL FRIENDSHIP'? THE GERMAN ALLIANCE, WAR AND MUSSOLINI'S DOWNFALL

1 C. Lowe and F. Marzari: *Italian Foreign Policy 1870–1940* (London: Routledge & Kegan Paul, 1975), p. 315.
2 R.J.B. Bosworth: *Mussolini* (London: Arnold, 2002), p. 350.
3 *Ciano's Diary 1939–1943* (ed. M. Muggeridge) (London: Heinemann, 1947), p. 125.
4 M. Knox, 'Expansionist Zeal, Fighting Power and Staying Power in the Italian and German dictatorships', in R. Bessel (ed.): *Fascist Italy and Nazi Germany: Comparisons and Contrasts* (Cambridge: Cambridge University Press, 1996), p. 168.
5 M. Robson: *Italy: Liberalism and Fascism 1870–1945* (London: Hodder & Stoughton, 1992), p. 134.
6 M. Blinkhorn: *Mussolini and Fascist Italy* (London: Methuen, 1984), p. 33.
7 Robson: op. cit., pp. 134–5.
8 S.P. MacKenzie: *The Second World War in Europe* (London: Longman, 1999), p. 31.
9 Bosworth: op. cit., p. 379.
10 A. Cassels: *Fascist Italy* (London: Routledge, 1977), p. 101.
11 MacKenzie: op. cit., p. 107.
12 Bosworth: op. cit., p. 30.
13 F.W. Deakin: *The Brutal Friendship: Mussolini, Hitler and the Fall of Italian Fascism* (London: Phoenix Press, 2000), p. 222.
14 Ibid: p. 223.
15 T. Abse, 'Italian Workers and Italian Fascism', in Bessel: op. cit., pp. 57–8.
16 Ibid: p. 59.
17 Deakin: op. cit., p. 110.
18 Ibid: pp. 112–14.
19 D. Mack Smith: *Italy and its Monarchy* (New Haven: Yale University Press, 1989), p. 305.
Source A: *Ciano's Diary*, op. cit., p. 79.
Source B: Quoted in Lowe and Marzari: op. cit., p. 409.
Source C: *Ciano's Diary*, op. cit., p. 411.
Source D: Quoted in Lowe and Marzari: op. cit., p. 413.
Source E: Quoted in Deakin: op. cit., p. 364.
Source F: Quoted in R. Klibansky (ed.): *Mussolini Memoirs 1942–1943* (London: Phoenix Press, 2000), pp. 65–6.
Source G: Quoted in J. Whittam: *Fascist Italy* (Manchester: Manchester University Press, 1995), p. 167.
Source H: Quoted in Klibansky: op. cit., p. 81.

## 8. FASCISM AND NAZISM

1   R. Pearce: *Fascism and Nazism* (London: Hodder & Stoughton, 1997), pp. 48–50.
2   Quoted in C. Delzell (ed.): *Mediterranean Fascism, 1919–1945* (New York: Harper & Row, 1970), p. 104.
3   E. Nolte: *Three Faces of Fascism* (London: Weidenfeld & Nicolson, 1965).
4   S. Payne: *A History of Fascism 1919–1945* (London: UCL Press, 1999).
5   Quoted in R. Eatwell, 'What is Fascism', *History Review* 26, December 1996, p. 30.
6   F.L. Carsten: *The Rise of Fascism* (London: Batsford, 1982), pp. 10–11, 230.
7   R. Eatwell: *Fascism, a History* (London: Vintage Press, 1995), p. xix.
8   Ibid: p. xxii.
9   R. Griffin (ed.): *Fascism* (Oxford: Oxford University Press, 1995).
10   Ibid: pp. 17–18.
11   Quoted in R.J.B. Bosworth: *The Italian Dictatorship. Problems and Perspectives in the Interpretation of Mussolini and Fascism* (London: Arnold, 1998), p. 75.
12   Griffin: op. cit., p. 79.
13   Quoted in Bosworth: op. cit., p. 23.
14   Bosworth, op.cit., p. 297.
15   Pearce, op.cit., p. 86.
Source A: Quoted in J. Whittam: *Fascist Italy* (Manchester: Manchester University Press, 1995), p. 163–4.
Source B: Quoted in Griffin: op. cit., p. 84.
Source C: Eatwell: op. cit., 1995, p. 67.
Source D: D. Mack Smith: *Mussolini* (London: Phoenix Press, 1998), p. 221.
Source E: R.J.B. Bosworth: *Mussolini* (London: Arnold, 2002), p. 344.

# SELECT BIBLIOGRAPHY

There are a number of readable and accessible books on Italy between the wars. Among the most rewarding are M. Robson's *Italy, Liberalism and Fascism 1870–1945* (London, 1992), which is particularly useful on Italy's pre-1914 problems as well as containing advice on note-taking, essay-writing and source-based questions; M. Blinkhorn: *Mussolini and Fascist Italy* (London, 1984), a concise summary of the key issues; J. Pollard: *The Fascist Experience in Italy* (London, 1998), which contains a number of documentary sources as does J. Whittam: *Fascist Italy* (Manchester, 1995). C. Delzell (ed.): *Mediterranean Fascism 1919–1945* (New York, 1970), is also an invaluable source of the kinds of documentary material likely to appear on examination papers.

Also useful are P. Morgan: *Italian Fascism 1919–1945* (Basingstoke, 1995), A. Cassels: *Fascist Italy* (London, 1977), and the section on inter-war Italy in M. Clark: *Modern Italy* (London, 1984). General books on Fascism such as F.L. Carsten: *The Rise of Fascism* (London, 1982), and R. Eatwell: *Fascism, a History* (London, 1995), also have sections on Italy.

Much more detailed and covering only part of the period are A. Lyttelton: *The Seizure of Power: Fascism in Italy 1919–1929* (London, 1973), and C. Seton-Watson: *Italy from Liberalism to Fascism 1870–1925* (London, 1972).

The two best biographies of Mussolini are D. Mack Smith: *Mussolini* (London, 1998), and the recently published R.J.B. Bosworth: *Mussolini* (London, 2002).

## ECONOMY AND SOCIETY

Compared with the plethora of research in this area on Nazi Germany, little has as yet been published in English on Italian society under Fascism. The most informative work is still E.R. Tannenbaum: *Fascism in Italy – Society and Culture 1922–45* (London, 1972). Alternatively there are chapters incorporating recent research, for example on the working class and on women, in R. Bessel (ed.): *Fascist Italy and Nazi Germany, Comparisons and Contrasts* (Cambridge, 1996).

## FOREIGN POLICY AND WAR

All the general books on Fascist Italy have sections on this, though some deal with it rather perfunctorily. D. Mack Smith: *Mussolini's Roman Empire* (Harmondsworth, 1976), is still the most informative coverage of foreign policy. Published primary sources include *Ciano's Diaries 1937–1938* and *1939–1943* (London, 1952 and 1947 respectively); also C. Lowe and F. Marzari: *Italian Foreign Policy 1870–1940* (London, 1975). *Mussolini's Memoirs* (London, 2000), written in the Salò Republic, provide interesting, though rambling, reminiscences about policy during the war, his relations with the King, and his removal from power. F.W. Deakin: *The Brutal Friendship: Mussolini, Hitler and the Fall of Italian Fascism* (London, 1962), is an authoritative source for German–Italian relations and Italy's role in the war, and covers the period from 1942 to 1945, but it is far too lengthy and detailed to be of much value to students.

## THEORIES OF FASCISM

This is a difficult topic and also a controversial one among historians. The main arguments are summarized in readable form in R. Pearce: *Fascism and Nazism* (London, 1997). In addition, R.J.B. Bosworth: *The Italian Dictatorship. Problems and Perspectives in the Interpretation of Mussolini and Fascism* (London, 1998), is a stimulating and thought-provoking work covering the historiography of Fascist Italy though it does demand some prior knowledge on the part of the student.

## ARTICLES

Lastly, there are some excellent articles on Fascist Italy. These include: J. Whittam: 'Mussolini, the Man "Sent by Providence"', *Modern History Review* 8, February 1997; J. Whittam: 'The Quest for Strong Leadership in Italy Led to the Identification of Mussolini as a Messiah Figure', *New Perspective* 3, March 1998; and P. Morgan: 'The Historiography of Fascist Italy', *New Perspective* 6, March 2001.

# INDEX